To Jerry

in friendship + freedom

Ry

B

Beyond

Beyond Lowu Bridge

Beyond Lowu Bridge

Roy Cheng Tsung

一线之隔

First Edition 2014
Published in the United States of America
Printed by Spencer Printing

Publisher's Cataloging-In-Publication Data
(Prepared by The Donohue Group, Inc.)

Tsung, Roy Cheng.
  Beyond Lowu Bridge / Roy Cheng Tsung. -- First edition.

    pages ; cm

    ISBN: 978-0-9836209-5-2

    1. Tsung, Roy Cheng--Travel--China. 2. Chinese Americans--Biography.
3. China--Social conditions--1949-1976. 4. China--History--1949-1976. 5.
Communism--China--History--20th century. I. Title.

E184.C5 T78 2014
973.04951

Passager Books is in residence at the University of Baltimore
in the School of Communications Design.

Passager Books
1420 North Charles Street
Baltimore, Maryland 21201
www.passagerpress.com

Beyond Lowu Bridge

Roy Cheng Tsung

Passager Books
Baltimore, MD
2014

In memory of my father
Wei-hsien Tsung 宗惟贤
for his wisdom and strength
&
my mother
Julia Shun-ching Liao Tsung 廖舜琴
for her love and courage.

To my daughters
Kristine and Lauren
for whom this story is written.

PART 1 (1949-1961)

PART 2 (1966-1972)

PART 3 (1972-1974)

Author's Note

All the characters in the story are real. Many names have been changed or purposely omitted. For the most part, the names are spelled in the standard Pinyin romanization system used in mainland China today. The exceptions are my family name Tsung (宗 zong) and such old familiar names as Sun Yat-sen, Kuomintang, Chiang Kai-shek, Yangtze River, etc., which are spelled in the old Wade-Giles phonetics system.

The Chinese name 一线之隔 on the book cover is not a literal translation of the English title. It means "Separated by a Line."

Some parts of this book are based on the recollections of my mother, friends and relatives. The conversations are approximations of what was related to me. A few events appear out of exact chronology, but the story is set against an historical backdrop that many of us have lived through.

Prologue

"Y ou are an American citizen because you were born in New York," my father said to me one day. "But in the eyes of the Chinese law, if your father is Chinese, you are Chinese." I was not in the least interested in the judicial principles of determining a child's citizenship. At twelve, my world consisted of reading comic books and swapping bubble gum cards with my pals in Riverside Park.

"Superman?" my father asked, raising his eyebrow and stressing the first two syllables, as he noticed the comic book lying on my bed. "Who is he?"

"A man of steel from Planet Krypton," I said. As a rule, my

parents spoke to me in Mandarin. But since my Chinese vocabulary was limited, I was allowed to use English on such occasions. "He uses his superhuman powers to save people and fight crooks."

"Indeed? An extraterrestrial being helping to keep law and order on Earth?" my father replied in English with a comical grin on his face. "What sort of superhuman feats can he perform?"

"Lifting skyscrapers and seeing through walls."

"Superman . . . " mused my father as he picked up one of my comics, stroking his chin and flipping through the pages. "No imagination," he said, shaking his head theatrically.

"What do you mean?" I asked, slightly offended.

"Have I ever told you the legend of Sun Wu-Kung? He's the Chinese version of your superhero, except he was a monkey from our own planet Earth."

That night after dinner, he began the story of the famous Monkey King from a sixteenth century Chinese folk novel *Journey to the West*. Monkey King's magic cudgel could shrink into a tiny pin, or expand into a giant pillar. I was captivated by Sun Wu-kung's ability to perform dozens of transformations. Once he turned himself into a wayside shrine, transforming his mouth into the entrance, his teeth into doors, his tongue into a Buddhist monk, and his eyes into windows.

"Guess what happened to his tail?" said my father.

"Turned into a tree?"

"No," he chuckled. "He stuck it straight up and changed it into a flag pole! Now that's what I call original!"

Thus started the colorful bedtime adventures of Monkey King, as my father and I traveled to the faraway land of our ancestral China.

I had no idea then that within a few years, my father would move our family back to that faraway land, to what he believed to be "New China." But the land I knew from my father's stories about Monkey King turned out to be quite different from what I had imagined it to be. And contrary to my assumptions that I would grow up in America, I would become one of the few Chinese American youths to be transplanted to China at the height of the Cold War.

Part 1

1949-1961

chapter 1
The Letter

was born in Upper Manhattan in 1941, the year of the Pearl Harbor attack. But my father was a Chinese diplomat always on the move, and for the first eight years of my life, I lived in the U.S., Mexico, Canada and the Philippines. I never set roots anywhere. In late November 1949, we were living in the Philippines when my father received a letter from his youngest brother, my Seventh Uncle. He wrote to my father that the Communists had seized mainland China. The letter was mailed in care of my Fifth Uncle in Hong Kong so as not to arouse the suspicions of the Chinese Nationalist circles in Manila.

"The Chiang Kai-shek reactionary regime is overthrown," wrote my Seventh Uncle. "Our country is no longer in the hands of foreign imperialists." He boasted about New China and urged my father to return.

This letter was the call of my father's homeland. He beamed when he showed it to my mother.

My mother had never been interested in politics, but the letter smelled of propaganda. "You and your brother have not spoken or written to each other for years," she pointed out. "How odd he suddenly writes to you now. How do you know the letter isn't someone else's idea?"

The exuberant look on my father's face fell. There was a change in him and for days he looked like a man searching for something. For the first time, I saw lines on his forehead. He stopped playing chess and table tennis with me, and the paper kite we had made together lay in my closet. The letter wasn't mentioned again.

My father was not sure what to do. He needed time to learn more about the new situation in China. But it was too risky to go about this in the Philippines, where the Chinese community was mostly pro-Nationalist. A month later, he arranged for my mother and me to return to New York City, and he resigned from the consulate service soon after.

My parents married in Shanghai in 1935 and moved to New York City where my father was Chinese Vice Consul.

Chapter 2
Uninvited Guests

y mother and I were living on 110th Street, an old neighborhood across from Riverside Park, when my father joined us in New York City. Our lifestyle had changed significantly. No more maids or servants, no cars or chauffeurs. My mother, who never had to work for a living before, was now assembling beads and pasting jewels for Midtown Jewelry Novelty, a small company in downtown Manhattan. Every morning, she would catch a subway train to Herald Square Station and trudge along the Avenue of the Americas to West 36th Street. We could only afford to rent a single room with a small kitchen. We shared a dingy bathroom down the hall with all the tenants on our floor. When it was our turn to use the shower, my mother would put on rubber gloves and scrub the shower stall first. I could feel her frustration, although she was braving it all with dignity.

I attended Public School 165, two blocks from our home. After school, I often dropped by Woolworth's Five-and-Dime at the corner of 110th and Broadway. If I had enough coins in my pocket, I would buy a little toy soldier for my collection. Next to Woolworth's, there was a store with roasting chickens on display. My mouth watered as I watched the chickens rotate slowly in the window oven, gravy dripping to the bottom pan.

One evening, Mary Davis, an old friend of my parents, joined us for dinner. Following the Chinese custom, I always called her Aunt Mary.

She and my father often had friendly debates about current events. They enjoyed the different cultural perspectives each had to offer: Aunt Mary, a red-headed heartland American from Oklahoma, and my father, the Chinese diplomat from ancient Beijing.

I was describing a lecture on the American presidential election system given by my fifth grade teacher, Mr. Spears, and I used the term "buttonholing."

"What is buttonholing?" my father asked. He loved colorful words and phrases.

"Oh, it's just an expression we use for trying to get someone's attention in conversation," said Aunt Mary.

"Mr. Spears said it was to grab someone's attention while trying to convince him to vote for you," I explained. "Mr. Spears says it's democracy at work."

My father was charmed. "This can only happen in the West."

Aunt Mary chuckled. "I wouldn't be so sure about the power of buttonholing – we do have our problems in the West," she said, with a twinkle in her eye.

My father laughed and said something about the naiveté of the East and West in the understanding of each other.

In October 1950, China intervened in the Korean War, supporting North Korea against the United States. The killing of Chinese soldiers was reported day after day in newspapers, radio broadcasts, and newsreels. The streets in my neighborhood overflowed with war comics. On my way to school, a group of teenagers called me names with racial slurs. Even the superintendent of our apartment building threw dark looks at me. We learned later that his son was on the Korean front.

My father left to work as a translator on the West Coast at the Hoover Research Institute. He also taught Mandarin Chinese at the Monterey Army Language School. To earn extra money, he even did some gardening work in Palo Alto and washed dishes in San Francisco's Chinatown. While he was in San Francisco, he befriended a group of patriotic Chinese scientists who had been educated in the United States and were seeking repatriation. He joined their activities to learn more about the situation in mainland China. His intentions were honest, but his activities would soon attract attention.

One evening, my mother was preparing supper and I was in the middle of my math homework when we heard a knock on the door. Two clean-shaven men in gray suits lifted their broad-brimmed hats.

"Mrs. Tsung?" asked the taller of the two.

"Yes," nodded my mother.

He opened his coat and flashed a shiny badge. "FBI. We have a couple of questions. May we come in, ma'am?"

The FBI agents interviewed my mother while I waited in the kitchen, eavesdropping through a small opening in the wooden swinging door. One asked the questions while the other took notes. I did not understand what was happening. Their dark neckties, somber gray suits, shiny black shoes, monotone voices and grim faces stuck in my memory cells.

After the agents left, my mother swept through the kitchen door with tears in her eyes. Her voice quivered with apprehension.

"It's all Qi Shu's fault," she said as I helped her to a chair.

"Who's Qi Shu?" I asked.

"Your Seventh Uncle."

For a moment, we sat tense and speechless in the small kitchen. I was numb all over, but I could feel my mother's anguish and pain.

"Why were they here?" I finally asked.

"They wanted to know why your father wants to return to China."

"What did you say?"

"I said my husband loves his country. I don't think they were satisfied with my answer though."

"Who's Owen Lattimore?" I asked.

"You were eavesdropping."

"I couldn't help it," I said, feeling foolish and embarrassed.

"He is a distinguished China scholar at Johns Hopkins University. A couple of years ago, there was something in the newspaper about him. He was accused of spying for the Soviet Communists."

"The Russians?" I gasped. At Booker T. Washington Junior High, we were taught that the Russians were preparing to drop the A Bomb on New York City. We had bomb drills, sometimes ducking under our desks in the classroom with our hands covering our faces; or kneeling in the corridor with our faces pressed against the floor; or curling ourselves under white sheets that were supposed to deflect radiation from the Russian Bomb. We even wore dog tags that were made to withstand a melting point of 1400 degrees Celsius and would be used to identify us in case our young bodies got incinerated by the Russian atomic blast. The mere mention of the word "Russian" drove a chill through my bones.

"Your father does not know this man, Owen Lattimore. Not at all," said my mother reassuringly. I felt relieved.

"I heard a couple of Chinese names. Who are they?" I asked.

"Chinese scientists your father met in San Francisco."

"Are they spies or something?"

"No, my son," sighed my mother. "They are just compatriots who want to return to China like your father."

"Why did Father get a sudden desire to return to China?"

"It all started because of your Seventh Uncle's letter," replied my mother with a trace of resentment in her hushed voice. She paused. "But he wasn't the only one who influenced your father."

"Who?"

"Remember Dr. Wang?"

"Yes," I said. "Wasn't he the one who came to dinner one

evening?"

"He's the one," she nodded. "Your father met him in San Francisco."

I grabbed a peanut cake from my mother's Chinese pastry box and settled back in my chair for the story.

"Dr. Wang Liang-jung was among the group of Chinese scientists your father became friends with in a YMCA hotel in Chinatown. Like your father, Dr. Wang saw a new day dawning for his country. He had made his first attempt to return to China by sea but got stopped in Honolulu by the U.S. Government. Your father must have been impressed by Dr. Wang's intrepid act. They became good friends."

It was growing dark. Silence filled our kitchen, save for the sound of the spoon against the pan as my mother made her stir-fried spinach.

"Was there anyone else?"

A thin line appeared on her forehead. My mother was about thirty-nine. Her hair was jet black. For a second, her porcelain face turned old.

"I don't know," she said. "But I have my suspicions."

I started to say something when she glanced at the clock.

"Let's have dinner," she said.

At first, I thought it was one of my father's weekly long-distance calls from San Francisco, so I waited for my turn. But I perked up when I heard my mother cry "Please think it over!"

I jumped to my feet and rushed to my mother's side. She was clenching the receiver, eyes red. She gripped my hand. "Here's your father," she said. "He wants a word with you."

"Little Cheng," my father began in an even tone, "listen carefully now. I am leaving for China tomorrow. You are twelve years old – practically a young man. Be brave now. I am counting on you to take care of Mom while I am away."

"But, but why?" I stammered.

"China needs us. There is a bright future there. I will write to you when I arrive in Beijing, and soon we will be together again. Now, please, let me talk to Mom."

I handed the phone back to my mother. Years later she told me that he had spoken to her of his obligation to China, that the "united front policy" meant the Chinese Government would welcome all compatriots returning to the Motherland.

"One more thing," he had said. "No passport for our son, even if the U.S. Immigration Office offers help."

"Fine," my mother had agreed resentfully. "But I am going to bring Little Cheng's birth certificate."

My birth certificate could have complicated things, but my mother was determined. It would be the single piece of paper in a faraway land that could tie me to my country of birth. To this day, I am very thankful for my mother's foresight and her determination to hang on to it. So it was arranged that he would write to her from Beijing, and we were to take the next available ship.

"China is his calling, Julia. He has to go," Aunt Mary said to my mother, who was upset about my father's unilateral decision. She had invited us to her apartment for lunch and was trying to comfort my mother.

"All our relatives and friends tried to talk him out of it," my mother said as she dabbed her eyes with a small handkerchief.

"I know," said Aunt Mary. "I tried, too. I even showed him a *Time* magazine article about Chinese labor camps and public executions. But he dismissed it with a wave of his hand and said 'How absurd!' He conceded that such cruelty probably existed in Soviet Russia under Stalin, but 'not in civilized China.'"

S.S. President Cleveland, "California to the Orient"

Chapter 3
Farewell

n the day of our departure from New York, Aunt Mary drove us to the Grand Central Terminal.

She pulled out a piece of paper and handed it to my mother. "My address," she said. "Let's keep in touch."

"We can write to each other in care of my sister Grace in Hong Kong," my mother said. The Korean War had ended, but not the hostility between China and the United States. Letters to and from mainland China were censored on both sides.

"It's perfectly all right with me if you write to me directly," Aunt Mary said reassuringly. "I want especially to hear from Little Cheng."

Our relatives were waiting for us at the information booth in the huge main hall. I craned my neck to gaze at the high ceiling depicting the constellations of the zodiac. The vast shiny floor was bustling with human activity.

"Remember to tell Lao Tsung that the Communists trust nobody except their own party members," said Granduncle Lin to my mother as we approached a long train of olive drab passenger cars. We were bound for San Francisco where we would take the *S. S. President Cleveland* to Hong Kong, and from there we would cross the border into Communist China.

"All aboard," announced the conductor. The moment had come. I was suddenly overwhelmed with sadness and anxiety. Aunt Mary gave me a big hug. "I promise to write to you if you promise too," she said.

I nodded my head, climbed the steps to our Pullman car, and bid farewell.

On the afternoon of November 5, 1953, my mother and I arrived at Pier 60 in San Francisco and boarded the *President Cleveland*, a white and gray ocean liner with two tall dark blue smokestacks bearing the red and white emblem of the American President Line. With a heavy heart, I followed my mother down the winding stairs into the hull of the ship where third class accommodations were located. We were quartered in different rooms.

There was one trifling but unforgettable incident before the ship raised anchor. I shared a compartment with a group of elderly men and one young man who was chatting with them in a strange nasal-sounding language that defied my comprehension. Since I had the upper berth, I had put my suitcase underneath the bunk below mine. Suddenly one of the old men yanked out my suitcase and pushed it aside. At first, I thought he wanted the whole space for himself; but after realizing that he had only a small bag, I carefully replaced my suitcase under his bunk.

Again, he shoved it aside. "What's wrong?" I asked, first in English and then in Mandarin Chinese. To my dismay, the old man did not understand a word I was saying. He stared at me and muttered something. His dark suntanned face was wrinkled, and one could tell that he had worked with his hands all his life.

"He doesn't understand English or Mandarin. He speaks a local dialect of Guangdong Province," the young man explained in English as he rose from his bunk. "He thinks you're Japanese. He and his companions are returning from Cuba to their home villages. His whole family was murdered by the Japanese during the War."

In my childhood, I had learned from my parents and relatives about the atrocities committed during the Japanese invasion in China. I remembered their conversations about the Nanjing Massacre. But my parents never taught me to hate. Once, my mother donated a bag of clothes to a Japanese nurse living on our apartment floor. "But she's Japanese," I protested. My mother replied, "She is not guilty of the war. She is just a fellow human being like you and me." My encounter with the old man was an eye opener. I was now aware of something called *minzu chouhen* – national hatred.

Fortunately, I had learned to write my name in Chinese. The old man regarded me with suspicion, but finally nodded his head.

A whistle sounded. It was 4:45 p.m. The ship suddenly came alive and I felt a gentle throb against the soles of my shoes. My mother and I climbed up the stairs to the deck to witness the departure. Horns and whistles were blowing full blast while passengers waved to their loved ones on shore. Many started to sing "Auld Lang Syne," and some threw long strips of colored paper from the deck to people on the dock. I hugged my mother as the pier and landscape slid by. We only had each other on the ship. Our friends and relatives had seen us off at New York City's Grand Central Station. Here, there was no one to wave us farewell.

Soon the Golden Gate Bridge appeared. This was not a dream, I told myself. It was really happening. I grasped the railing as we sailed under the Golden Gate, and for a long time I watched the bridge slowly fade into the distance.

As the *Cleveland* set course for the high seas, the beat of the engine increased and the ship started to roll, leaving a churning white wake which faded quickly into the blue waters of the broad Pacific. I trained my eyes on the distant shoreline and watched it slowly disappear.

Chapter 4
Lowu Bridge

ovember 21, 1953. After sixteen days at sea, I peeked out of the porthole. The early morning sky was tinted with streaks of red and gray clouds. Through the thin mist, I saw a faint outline of land on the horizon. Tiny islands stood out of the water like jagged rocks as the *S.S. President Cleveland* steered towards the port of Hong Kong.

A small motorboat sped towards our ship. The humming of the ship's engines ceased. The American liner stopped short of entering the harbor as the small craft pulled alongside. A loud thud and rattling sound vibrated throughout our third-class compartment walls as the crew opened the gangway and lowered a gangplank.

Minutes later, a squad of armed officers led by a tall British officer boarded the steamship. Some of them appeared to be Gurkha soldiers wearing battle fatigues and armed with rifles. They had come for the ten of us bound for Communist China. It was at the height of the Cold War and we were not allowed to set foot on Hong Kong soil.

We were summoned to the dining hall. The officers scrutinized our papers and escorted us to the gangway. Under the watchful eyes of the officers, we disembarked from the ship and found ourselves on a police launch manned by a constable in white and khaki. Laborers boarded the *Cleveland* for our luggage.

By now, the rest of the passengers had gathered on the deck. Many of them smiled and waved, while others stared. They looked so far away from where I sat petrified on the tiny police boat three stories below the ship's deck.

At the last minute, an unfortunate person was thrown into our group, a leathery-faced professional gambler. He had been deported from the United States and was on his way to Portuguese-controlled Macao. Just before we set off, he was shoved onto the gangway by the officers, and with a kick from behind, came tumbling down the plank and landed on our boat. A ripple of cruel laughter passed through the passengers watching from the deck of the *Cleveland*. Even we could not help laughing at the wretched gambler. He swore and shook his fists at the officers, in vain. He was trapped, bound for Communist China.

The gangplank was hoisted, the door closed, and the hull of the ship became a giant wall of riveted steel plates. I felt the vibration of the motor as our boat started to move. As a gap opened between the

President Cleveland and us, the massive steel wall began to slide past. Our little boat sped away to a desolate spot north of Hong Kong.

Like prisoners, we were quickly led onto a shabby train that was guarded by turbaned officers in police uniforms. They sat among us; I felt the tension in the atmosphere. Even I, a young boy, was placed under tight surveillance. When I asked permission to go to the washroom, one of them accompanied me there. He bolted the window and kept the door wide open.

"May I please have some privacy?" I ventured to ask. The officer stared at me for a moment. He was holding a menacing rifle, but looked a little friendlier than the others. "Perhaps we can leave the door slightly ajar," I said.

He nodded his head and looked the other way.

"Where you learn English?" he asked when I returned to my seat, trembling and tongue-tied.

"He was born in New York City," my mother answered for me.

He smiled at me, revealing tobacco-stained teeth. "You speak good English," he said with a heavy accent. "Don't forget English. You can make big money in China."

The other officers laughed. We said nothing. I wished we could turn back, but I had no choice. My father was already in Beijing waiting for us. I wondered if he was also treated like a fugitive. My mother held my hand in hers as our train continued northwards. I understood enough to know that I was being transplanted to a land that was still at war with my native-born country. "Why?" I kept asking myself. "Why am I on this train? Why did my father move to China?" As our train rumbled along the tracks, I closed my eyes, feeling the burden of my father's irreversible decision.

I felt a jolt and I opened my eyes. Our train came to a halt.

Barbed wire fences and a wooden bridge came into view as my mother and I got off the train with our fellow passengers.

"Lowu Bridge," someone murmured.

The bridge was not long. It was a simple structure of wood and concrete with railway tracks. A white demarcation line ran across the middle. There were no modern buildings on the Chinese side. The land looked barren and rural. Behind the Chinese border guards, a five-star red flag fluttered from the top of its tall staff.

We were promptly marched off to a small outpost structure near the checkpoint and lined up against the wall. A grim British officer with dark glasses came out and looked us over. Across Lowu Bridge stood solemn Chinese guards in olive green. One of them was holding a large automatic weapon with holes in the barrel.

I reluctantly followed my mother across the bridge. Two People's Liberation Army guards came forward. I heard a voice addressing us over a loudspeaker. "Welcome countrymen!" it said, followed by a song that began with "East is red, the sun rises." My mother surrendered her passport. It had a red diplomatic cover and bore the Chinese Nationalist Government emblem.

I looked over my shoulder and glanced back at the other end of the bridge. With fists on hips, the grim British officer stood beneath the Union Jack, observing us through his dark glasses. Behind him, the armed men remained at attention. I looked for the officer with tobacco-stained teeth. For a second, there was a faint smile on his dark face when our eyes met. As I stood on the small wooden bridge, I stole one last glimpse of the outside world.

五

Chapter 5
The Poster

y mother and I hardly exchanged any words as we sat among strangers on board the train from subtropical Guangzhou to wintry Beijing. Cinders from the trailing smoke of the locomotive snapped against the windows. When our train reached the flat plains of Northern China, a sandstorm gusted in and the temperature grew colder and colder as we approached our final destination.

Our train pulled into Qianmen Railway Station. It was already dark in Beijing. A pocket of freezing air burst into the compartment when the conductor opened the door. Outside, we were greeted by the puffing sound of steam billowing from the locomotive engine.

As I stepped onto the poorly lit platform, my eyes fell on a large propaganda poster. It featured a huge fist crushing a group of puny green-faced figures. One looked like Uncle Sam with a battered stars-and-stripes hat; a couple of them looked like American G.I.s fleeing for their lives; and there was a fat, frock-coated creature with a fistful of U.S. dollars, presumably representing Wall Street capitalism. I shivered and clung to my mother's fur coat. The platform started to fill up as more passengers got off the train.

Just then, from the distance, I heard a familiar voice calling our names: "Shun Ching . . . Little Cheng . . . "

It was my father, a tall figure weaving through the crowd in our direction. We ran into each other's arms, kissing and hugging. His old American overcoat felt like a warm blanket. A dark blue scarf was wrapped around his neck. Vapor was pouring from his nostrils into the frigid air.

"It's so cold. Why aren't you wearing a hat?" chided my mother.

"Hat? Why yes, of course," replied my father, reaching into his coat pocket. Instead of his favorite broad-brimmed felt hat, he put on a strange blue cap. "Current fashion," he explained humorously.

For a moment, I thought I saw a man by the poster watching us. He was wearing an army green cotton-padded coat and hat with large earflaps. When he noticed me, he shifted his eyes and started to move.

In the dim light, I perceived a weak smile on my father's face. There was something different about him. He looked serious and considerably thinner, and there were dark circles around his eyes.

I looked for the man in green. He was gone.

Two large pedicabs were waiting for us outside the train station.

Unlike those in the South, pedicabs in Beijing had cotton-padded hoods over the passenger seats. After the passenger got in, the opening was sealed with thick canvas or a quilt to keep out the freezing wind. The pedicab drivers, who had to endure the harsh subzero winds, wore clumsy cotton-padded coats, trousers and shoes. Large padded gloves hung at their sides from a string around their necks. The northerners believed that "cold starts from the feet," so the drivers bound their legs with cloth tapes for extra protection.

My mother and I shared one pedicab; my father and the luggage, the other. As we pulled out of Qianmen Railway Station, I wondered about the poster and the man in green. I missed Riverside Park and my friends. I would've given anything to go back to our old apartment in New York. Even the dingy bathroom seemed better.

The pedicab stopped. I carefully pushed open the canvas and peeked outside. We were at an entrance leading into a compound of brick houses. My father was talking to the guard who opened the gate to let us in. Eventually, we arrived at a handsome two-story house. A middle-aged couple came to the door to greet us.

My father introduced us to his old schoolmate, Dr. Ho, and his wife. "You will be staying here overnight," he said to my mother and me.

Dr. Ho was a prominent surgeon at the famous Beijing Union Hospital Xiehe Yiyuan. He greeted me in English and inquired about our voyage.

"He speaks like an American," said Mrs. Ho.

"Of course." Dr. Ho smiled. "He was born in the United States." Patting me on the shoulder, the doctor said, "Keep up your English. You will need it."

It was getting late. My father had to leave. He was staying at the Returned Overseas Chinese Students Guest House in Fengsheng Hutong, a small alley tucked somewhere in the southwestern corner of the city.

"Please, can we go back home?" I pleaded as soon as my mother and I were left to ourselves. My mother put her arms around me and whispered gently, "I know that you are having a terrible time. So am I."

"But why?" I asked. "Why did we have to leave our home and come here?"

"Our country is no longer in the hands of foreigners. We are now our own sovereignty. Your father believes that there is a future here, especially for you."

"You're beginning to sound like Father," I said.

My mother sighed. "I wonder, too. But your father is a brilliant man. He sees far ahead, and I have to admit that this is over my head."

"You didn't really have to follow him here, did you?"

My mother bowed her head in thought. Looking up at me she said, "Your father is a good man. I am his wife. My place is with him."

I knew how much my father loved his country. But I thought of the huge fist in the anti-American propaganda poster. I also remembered the war comics in my Manhattan neighborhood. They were filled with cartoons of grim-faced Yankee soldiers smashing in the heads of bestial-looking Chinese and North Korean soldiers with rifle butts, blowing them to bits with hand grenades, and slaughtering them with machine guns, trench knives and flame throwers. I remembered being in a movie theater with my mother when a newsreel showed scenes of American napalm bombing and burnt corpses of Chinese soldiers. She got up, took my hand, and quietly led me outside. Although I was only twelve, I was old enough to feel the bitter hostility between China and the United States, and I could not help wondering how it would impact an American-born Chinese youngster growing up in Beijing.

Chapter 6

Year of the Horse

When we first arrived in Beijing, the oppressive fortress-like ancient walls still surrounded the city. I was bored by dull gray structures everywhere. I loathed the sand and dust that piled up on our windowsill and seeped through cracks and crevices into our small dwelling. I dreaded the long icy winters; the winds pierced through my cotton-padded coat and chilled me to the bones.

But this was my father's beloved hometown, the ancient city of winding, narrow unpaved alleys and lanes called *hutongs*. "There is no word in English for hutong," he explained with pride. "Even the word 'alley' doesn't quite measure up to it."

One day, we were strolling along an old dirt road outside Beijing City's Fucheng Gate. Worn-out mules harnessed to run-down carts wobbled by. The landscape on either side of the road was made up of shabby houses, shops and eating houses with equally raggedy-looking people dressed in the same shades of gray and black. "I know that China is poor and backward now," my father said. "But China will rise to be a modern nation. It is a big country with enormous potential power. That's why we brought you here. We want you to be a part of China's future."

We celebrated my first Chinese New Year, Year of the Horse, in Beijing with my father's bosom friend Uncle Wei and his family. I was a little confused. "But we just celebrated New Year's," I said.

"That was the Western calendar," my father explained. "We have our own, and all of our traditional festivals are still based on the lunar year."

"Why Year of the Horse?" I inquired.

"We have twelve favorite animals. Each year is named after one. When we think of the horse, we think of its loyalty, its intelligence and strength. We have a saying in Chinese: *Qianli Ma* – a horse that travels a thousand miles a day."

I thought of a great white stallion galloping across the plains of the Wild West with a masked cowboy on its back. "Hi-yo, Silver!" I said.

My father winked. "You see, even the Lone Ranger recognizes the energy and goodness of a horse like Silver."

We gathered in Uncle Wei's house for the New Year dinner. Aunty Wei placed a large fish dish prominently at the center of the round table. The meal had many courses. My favorite was dumplings filled with minced pork, finely chopped vegetables and garlic chives. Each dumpling was a sealed packet with all the goodies of the filling retained inside, juicy and tender, tasty and fragrant. Aunty Wei proudly brought out a Peking duck fresh from the oven. The shiny brown, thin, crispy skin was absolutely divine. It was served with pancakes, spring onions and sweet bean sauce. Uncle Wei got out a carving knife and sliced the duck in front of us just like a chef in the famous Quan Ju De Restaurant in the old city's Qian Men Street.

The last course was dessert. "Ah, glutinous rice cakes from the South!" exclaimed Uncle Wei, who was a northerner.

My mother's face lit up. "Yes. We always had them for New Year in my hometown down south."

Uncle Wei raised a cup of wine to my father. "Welcome home, Old Brother." And to everyone he said, "Happy Year of the Horse. May all of your wishes come true."

After dinner, I followed the kids outside. The courtyard was decorated with red and orange paper lanterns that shone brightly in the night. It was freezing, but the air was still and I could smell burning wax from the candles. Soon, we got down to business. Firecrackers! We loved the ancient New Year tradition of lighting firecrackers to scare away evil spirits. Happily for us, although evil spirits were frowned upon as feudalistic superstition in Communist China, firecrackers had not been banned.

The firecrackers were rolled up in heavy red paper and burst with deafening explosions. BANG, BANG, BANG!

Uncle Wei rushed out of the house. "Not in the courtyard! Let's do it outside."

Symmetrically built along the north-south axis, the entire housing compound was private, enclosed with a large, heavy gate at the entrance. The gate had a fresh coat of red paint. Two lanterns hung on either side of the entrance. Uncle Wei inserted one end of a long rod into a hole in the entrance post and hung up a string of braided firecrackers. Everyone stepped back as he lit the long fuse.

The crackers popped and banged in a series of blasts and flashes. The acrid smell of burning black powder filled my nostrils. The kids jumped up and down with glee.

"Look what I brought," exclaimed Little Four, a neighborhood boy. He pulled out a skyrocket.

"Hooray! Hooray!" we all yelled.

"Over there, please." Uncle Wei pointed to a spot away from the entrance and walls. Little Four planted the little skyrocket on the ground and we formed a circle around him as he lit the fuse. The tiny flare snaked its way along the fuse; Little Four plugged his ears just as the spark reached the rocket.

POW! The little rocket shot straight up into the air with a trail of sparks. Then, a distant pop, followed by several more. Red, orange, white and green sparkling shapes lit up high above in the starry sky and blossomed into magnificent chrysanthemums. Then laughter and the clapping of little hands. Cheers and hoorays. My father beamed with delight as he stood next to Uncle Wei.

For a moment, I forgot all about New York City.

My father's genuine love and passion for Beijing was infectious. Slowly I began to appreciate the graceful curve of roofs rising above the gray walls against the clear blue sky. And I enjoyed the gentle rustle of red autumn leaves as the smell of roasting chestnuts floated into our neighborhood with the cool breeze.

One morning, my father and I climbed aboard the only streetcar in Old Beijing, the Circle Route. As the ancient tram rumbled along the iron tracks, he pointed out places from his childhood. He took me to a small noodle house with a crowd of patrons lined up at the entrance. Steam rose from a large boiling pot and fogged the window.

"Watch the chef," my father said, pointing to a stout man pulling long strands of dough with his powerful hands. "He's the best in town." The noodles grew in length with each twist and pull, and multiplied in numbers with each fold. They were so fluffy and tasty, I was in heaven.

Towards the end of the day, we ended up in Dong Jiao Min Xiang. Known to the West as Foreign Legation Quarters, it was a lovely street with European style buildings on either side. As we were walking along the old pavement, my father said, "This place became a city within a city exclusively for foreigners following the 1900 Boxer Rebellion. There used to be a sign here that read 'No dogs, No Chinese allowed.'"

After a pause, he said, "Can you imagine such a sign on our own soil?"

As we passed by an old red brick building, he stopped again. "See that corner? That's where I saw a Chinese rickshaw man booted in the rear by a foreign soldier."

I stared at the spot.

"China was different when I was your age," said my father. "We were a weak nation then. We lost our sovereignty. A British gunboat could sail up and down the Yangtze River with impunity and dictate China's politics."

It was getting late. The streets were empty. "You will study Chinese history in school," he said. "You will learn about the Opium War of the 1840s and the beginning of China's humiliation at the hands of the British and other foreign powers."

Chapter 7
Seventh Uncle

i Shu was my father's seventh and youngest sibling. But no one could have guessed that they were brothers. They were complete opposites and hardly ever saw eye to eye. My father was tall and lean; Qi Shu was short and pudgy. My father was scholarly and detested politics; Seventh Uncle's whole life seemed to revolve around revolutions and party doctrines.

My first encounter with Seventh Uncle was shortly after our arrival in Beijing. The U.S. Seventh Fleet was deployed in the Taiwan Straits. I was naive and proudly showed my uncle a model ship I had made in New York. It was a U.S. battleship decorated with colorful signal flags. "It's a plastic model kit and I painted it myself," I explained. My Chinese vocabulary was limited, but Qi Shu knew enough English to understand me. At first he said nothing. He merely stared at the model.

I was about to give him a little history of the battleship when he asked me, "What is the significance of bringing this warship into our country?"

"Significance?" I blurted out. It was a big word and I had no idea where he was coming from. I shrugged my shoulders. "It's just a toy model."

"Do you know what this warship represents?"

"It's a U.S. naval battleship," I responded cautiously.

He looked dead serious, but bore no malice. "It's the warship of the American Imperialists, our Number One Enemy," he said.

I thought for a moment and replied, "This happens to be the model of the *U.S.S. Missouri.* The Japanese surrendered on this ship on September 2, 1945. At that time, China and the United States were allies."

My father, who was sitting by the window, smiled and gave me the thumbs up.

Qi Shu never mentioned the model again. But he frequently cautioned me against "bad" Western ideas and influences. He reminded me of a political commissar, and I kept a respectful distance from him. As the years went by and I continued to harbor what he considered "decadent" Western ideas, my uncle eventually gave up on me and I rarely saw him.

Chapter 8
School Behind Fences

The road was muddy and treacherous when my father and I first set out for Beijing Returned Overseas Chinese Preparatory School one December morning in 1953. It had snowed the previous day and our pedicabs would not go beyond Fucheng Men, one of the west gates of the old city.

"Bus stop's over there," said the driver, pointing to a red and yellow sign at the foot of the city wall where we boarded a rickety old American Dodge bus painted red and yellow, with only two benches on either side of the aisle.

As we slowly negotiated our way through the giant archway of

Fucheng Gate, the bus suddenly sputtered and stopped. Calling for help, the conductor dashed to the exit, followed by several young men. My father rose to his feet, but the driver motioned to him to remain seated. "Comrade," he smiled, "no need for your help. The young men will take care of it."

"Why did he call you 'comrade?'" I whispered.

My father thought for a moment. "It seems to be the common form of address nowadays. I guess it's because we're all working for the same cause."

I had no idea what my father meant by "cause," and I did not care either. My father had enrolled me in a special boarding school for ethnic Chinese students from foreign countries, and I was worried about the immediate prospect of being separated from my parents.

"Overseas Chinese School," announced the conductor. "This is where you get off."

A group of red brick buildings appeared behind a tall chain link fence, and an old man in an olive green cotton-padded coat emerged from a small booth to open the gate for us. His dark, wrinkled face was marked by a scar on his right temple, and he wore some sort of medal on his weather-beaten outfit. "Need to register first," he ordered in an unfamiliar, barely comprehensible accent. "No one enters or leaves without registration."

With that, my new school life began behind guarded fences.

"You seem to have no problem with spoken Chinese," said the

principal, our first stop in my enrollment. "How many Chinese characters can you read and write?"

I scratched my head in embarrassment. "About a hundred, I think."

The elderly man shook his head. "There are almost 50,000 characters in the famous *Kangxi Dictionary*, but you only need to master 7,000 basic ones in order to be admitted to high school. We'll have to put you in a beginner's class."

In Language Class Level One, I met Jean Su, an American girl about four or five years my senior.

"It looks like we're the only ones from the States," I said to her.

"That's for sure," she answered with a wink.

"Why the guard?" I asked, referring to the old man at the gate.

She shrugged. "During weekdays, we're only allowed outside the campus from five to six p.m."

"I can't wait to see my mom and dad this weekend," I said.

"You can leave after three on Saturday, but you have to be back by seven on Sunday evening."

My heart sank. "You mean we don't have a whole day off on Saturdays?"

Jean shook her head. "Afraid not. Political meetings in the morning and group discussions after lunch."

"What sort of meetings?"

She forced a wry smile. "Oh, you'll find out soon."

There was no need for her to spell it out. Although I was new in town, I already had a hunch, thanks to my Seventh Uncle, who had given me a good taste of ideology. Those of us who grew up in foreign countries were hopelessly "westernized," and had to be "remolded."

My first night on campus was one of sleepless twitching and rolling in a lower bunk next to the door. I was in a room of double-decker berths shared by seven strangers who spoke Mandarin with an odd guttural accent. They were from Jakarta, and much older than I was. I was confused and had not the faintest idea what my father meant by a bright future in China. The moon shone on our windowsill and cast an unrecognizable shadow on the floor. A train chugged by in the distance as I lay awake in the dark imagining myself on board, heading south for the border. I remembered the *President Cleveland*, its shiny decks and the feeling of freedom.

For meals, we would line up with chopsticks, spoons, bowls and aluminum containers in a large mess hall. Bamboo crates of steaming rice were rolled out. At that time, there was enough that we could go back for refills. The following year, the government started to ration rice and the crates disappeared. The dishes were bland and soggy; there would be days when nothing but eggplant was served with hardly any meat or no meat at all. Occasionally, the cooks would produce something palatable like braised meatballs and bean curd.

Across the dirt road, there was a family-run deli that must have made a fortune on chocolate bars, curry dumplings and pastries that were over-priced but very popular. For sixty minutes in the late afternoons, the shop became my refuge outside the chain link fences.

I hated the ideological meetings. I dreaded the long hours of nonsensical lectures about socialist virtues; I could not stand the endless denunciations of U.S. imperialism and the "decadent" West. Worse yet, I had to pretend to be a believer. I taught myself the art of meditation while appearing to be attentive at the meetings. To this day, I still cringe at the mere mention of the word "meeting."

I resented being reprimanded for the slightest "sin." There were opportunists in our midst who reported on others for their own advancement. The feeling of being scrutinized was intimidating. I felt like a dangerous species labeled *Born in the U.S.A.* under a giant magnifying glass.

One afternoon, I was summoned to my political instructor's room. He was assigned to guide me in correct ideological thinking, Marxism, Leninism and Maoism.

"I hear you read English books," he began. I had already been criticized for speaking "American imperialist" language. "Nonsense!" my father had exclaimed when I told him about it. "Tell them that language is created by the people . . . and that Joseph Stalin said so." I never knew where he got the quotation from, but it stopped the criticism.

"What are you reading?" asked the counselor.

I pulled out a soft cover book and handed it to him. It was *Born of the People* by Luis Taruc, a Communist leader who led the Hukbalahap guerrilla movement during the Japanese invasion of the Philippines. Fortunately, my counselor was an educated man. His manners were refined and he had a cultivated Zhejiang accent.

"I see." The corners of his mouth curled into a faint smile. "It is good that you are reading progressive books," he said. "But you should read Chinese. After all, that is why you are in this school."

I suspect that my father had another reason for putting me in this school. He probably intended to set me up as a *Huaqiao*, which means Overseas Chinese. To be a Huaqiao was both unfortunate and fortunate. Unfortunate in that Huaqiaos were generally regarded with suspicion and the locals saw them as ideologically backward and politically unreliable. Fortunate in that the Government was comparatively lenient towards Huaqiaos, who were allowed to correspond with overseas relatives and friends, and even keep some of their Western habits. On the streets of Beijing, one could immediately spot a Huaqiao by his glossy hair, skinny pants and Rolex watch.

Six months after my arrival at the school, I was passing by an open door in the dorm and heard laughter. A crowd was gathered around a young Caucasian man with an impressive mustache. He was holding a bowl and chopsticks, trying to pronounce *fanwan* (rice bowl) and *kuaizi* (chopsticks) in Mandarin. It was obvious he could not speak a word of Chinese, and his roommates were trying to teach him some basic vocabulary.

Alvin was a radio engineer from New Zealand; his father was a Chinese immigrant and his mother a New Zealander. Like many young ethnic Chinese, he had come to help build New China.

"How did you get into this country?" I asked my new friend.

"Showed them a picture of my father," he said. "I guess the picture made me a Chinese."

In September, we were joined by his friends from New Zealand, Alex and York, who were brothers and spoke a little Cantonese. We were assigned the same dorm room and it became an instant gathering place for English-speaking friends. We organized chess tournaments on weekends and played against schoolmates from Holland, South Africa and the Soviet Union. We were stamp collectors and started a small "trading post." I began to enjoy dorm life. Our room had become a tiny oasis in a Socialist desert.

Near our dormitory was the school clinic, staffed by an old doctor and a young nurse. From his old army uniform, it was not difficult to surmise that the doctor was an army veteran from Shaanxi Province who had probably followed the Red Army into Beijing. Someone suggested that he was really a veterinarian. Whatever illness or malady a patient might be suffering from, he always prescribed a little white packet of APC, a kind of aspirin, or sulfa tablets. The students, however, had little confidence in the old doctor and often tossed the tablets.

One day, Alex appeared with two jumbo jars of APC and sulfa tablets. For weeks, he had been collecting discarded white packets all over the campus.

"What's it for?" I asked.

"New Year's Eve party," he answered with a mischievous grin.

When New Year's Eve arrived, the school assembled in a large hall to celebrate with music and plays prepared by students who carefully adhered to the politically-correct line. The teachers sang Chinese revolutionary songs accompanied by flute and accordion.

We had also prepared a show. When it was our turn, Jean, the emcee, announced, "Comrades, we have an emergency!" and pointed to my friend William, who was sitting in the audience. He suddenly clutched his stomach and groaned.

The room roared with laughter when Alex and York, dressed in surgical masks and white gowns, came running into the hall with a stretcher and whisked the patient away.

Meanwhile, Alvin and I slipped backstage to set up our equipment for a shadow show. The lights went off. I switched on my bicycle light to project the silhouettes of two doctors hovering over a patient lying on an operating table against a large white screen.

"This is bad," one doctor said. He whipped out a knife and ordered, "Put him to sleep."

The audience burst out laughing when the other doctor knocked the patient out cold with a hammer. The surgeons used knives, chisels and saws, complete with sound effects as, one by one, organs made of cardboard were removed and projected against the large screen, producing giggles and chortles among the spectators. We had prepared thick ropes for the "intestines." The sawbones tugged and pulled. Finally, two objects dangled at the end of the rope.

"What's this?" asked one of the doctors.

"Jars," replied the other. Holding up the jars, he came out from behind the screen and announced, "APC and sulfa tablets prescribed by the school clinic."

The room dissolved into laughter. The curtains dropped. Everyone except the school authorities rose from their seats and gave a standing ovation.

The next day, we were reprimanded for putting on a show that was tantamount to an "inappropriate attack" on the school doctor, who had a glorious revolutionary past.

I do not know if this was written into my record. But our play is still vivid in my imagination.

I was leaving my dorm one morning when I heard someone call my name through a window. It was Alvin. He signaled me to come to his room. At first, I barely recognized him. He had shaved off his mustache.

"What's up?" I asked.

A moment of silence.

"Going home."

I stared at him, not comprehending what he was saying. I could not imagine anyone leaving the country. "New Zealand?" I finally blurted out.

Alvin nodded his head.

It was the last time I saw him. But it was also the first time I realized that Huaqiaos could leave the country, and for many years I clung to this hope.

Chapter 9
Behind the Drum Tower

y family took up residence in a small and peaceful hutong behind the Drum Tower when my father was assigned to teach English, French and Spanish at the Beijing Institute of Foreign Trade. We had three rooms facing a large brick-laid courtyard shared by three households. At the center of the courtyard stood an old water tap which often froze at night in winter. At sunrise, the three families took turns pouring hot water on the faucet to restore the running water. The corner of our kitchen and dining space was occupied by a large earthen vessel that held our water supply.

Our coal stove was a constant test of patience and skill. In late fall, my father and I would set it up in the middle of the living and study room. The chimney, which had to be assembled from pipes of double-layer tin, extended upward toward the ceiling and across the room to a small opening in the window. The tin rusted and collected soot, which made it difficult for us to connect the pipes. One year, they were so rusty and out of shape that I was ready to give up.

"Get a soap bar," my father instructed. He rubbed one end of a pipe with the soap and said, "Try it now."

Sure enough, the two pipes connected perfectly.

"Learned it from a carpenter in San Francisco," my father chuckled.

"On a tin chimney?" I asked.

"No. On a stubborn screw."

Neither of us being mechanically inclined, we were proud of the result; and we were especially pleased with the success of the American remedy on the ancient Chinese chimney.

The peace and quiet of our neighborhood was occasionally broken by the sound of soft, highly musical cries of hawkers, often accompanied by clappers or hand gongs. Each peddler had his own distinctive way of advertising his merchandise or service. Some announced themselves with a small hand-drum with little metal beads at the sides; as the handle was twisted, the beads swung around and hit the drum in quick succession.

One Sunday afternoon we heard a different sound. It was a high-pitched note emitted from some sort of metallic instrument. "A traveling barber," my father declared. I strained my ears and scratched my head.

"If you don't believe me," he laughed, "go and see for yourself."

As I stepped outside, a man holding a large tuning fork passed by with a basin of hot water on a stove at one end of his shoulder pole and a stool for his client on the other. The knee-high stove was shaped like a barrel with four stubby legs on the bottom.

"Scissors and razors are probably in the stool," said my father, pointing to the small drawers with tiny copper handles. As the man continued on his way, he sounded the tuning fork again and cupped his ears, as if having the perfectly pitched note would help broadcast the announcement.

About a year later, we moved to South Peace Lane outside Anding Gate. My father's school had acquired several two-story buildings for faculty and staff housing. It was an improvement, for now we had the conveniences of a modern plumbing system and running water, and I could gaze out of the window to take in the scenery from high up. There was no central heating though; our Old German Stove moved in with us. The chimney pipes came too, along with rust and soot, and the soap bar.

During the Great Famine years from 1958 to 1962, we all watched food disappear from shops, and witnessed friends and neighbors suffer from malnutrition. Every day, my mother felt my neck and forehead with her fingers to see if there were any swollen spots from malnutrition. Meat became hard to find and unaffordable for many city dwellers. Then fruit dwindled down to small piles of wormy and rotten apples. Grain, which had already been rationed several years prior to the famine, was now even more limited in supply. Rice was so scarce that we had to cook porridge with what little we were able to buy. Sometimes we scraped the bottom of the pot for charred rice. "It actually tastes like *guo ba*," my father joked, referring to the baked rice patties in sizzling rice soup. But the burnt rice tasted bitter.

When our relatives in Hong Kong found out about our situation, they came to our aid. One of my aunts mailed us cooking oil and canned food. Another aunt found a mainland Chinese agency that sold food coupons in exchange for foreign currency. There was a special outlet in downtown Beijing that honored the coupons. The scheme enabled the Chinese government to acquire much-needed foreign currencies. It was "business" at our expense. But our survival was all that mattered.

One day in the autumn of 1960, my aunt, my mother's elder sister, showed up at our door. She had traveled three days and three nights by rail from Fujian Province, switching two or three trains along the way. It had been more than a decade since my mother last saw her family, and almost seven years since she spoke in her native tongue. With tears in her eyes, my mother cried, "*Dua Jie*," meaning Big Sister in Amoy dialect.

"Now, now, let's not get emotional," replied my aunt stoically, but dabbed her eyes quickly with her handkerchief as she limped on her cane into our apartment. She was in her late forties, gray-haired but very active.

My aunt's eyes widened with disbelief when we brought her to the special outlet downtown. In Beijing, conditions were much better than in rural areas. "Mountains of food," she later described in a letter to her husband, who stayed behind in Fuzhou City.

My aunt had survived the Japanese aggression and civil wars. She also lived through natural disasters, but this was the worst. "You are so lucky to be in Beijing," she said. "Where I come from, we are lucky to have rice porridge with pickled vegetables. Many of my neighbors eat rice husks, and some even cook tree bark." For three weeks, my mother and aunt cooked and packed dried *rou song* (fluffy pork) into large tin containers for my aunt to bring home to her family. She had three growing boys to feed. But my uncle would tiptoe to the kitchen in the middle of the night and help himself to a spoonful or two.

"Such is human life," my mother would say to me in Chinese.

One winter, when I was sick in bed, she got up at the crack of dawn to buy a live chicken in a black market across the town. "Chicken broth will get you back on your feet again," she said. But my mother, who had always bought meat from the marketplace, could not bring herself to kill the bird. "When it wiggled in my hands, I knew I couldn't do it," she said. "I had to ask for our neighbor's help."

She would line up for groceries for hours, rain or shine, and all of her shopping was done on foot. The image of my short, petite mother carrying a twenty-pound sack of flour on her slender shoulders will linger in my memory forever. I can still see her, a middle-aged woman slightly bent under the weight while trudging miles through the snow.

Chapter 10
Dear Aunt Mary

aunt Mary kept her promise; she wrote to me by way of my mother's sister in Hong Kong. "May I please write to her?!" I pleaded. The thought of reconnecting with Aunt Mary and the outside world excited me.

"Yes, but mail your letter care of Aunt Grace," my father advised. "There's an anti-communist hysteria going on in the States," he explained, referring to the McCarthy witch hunts. Since my mother's sister Grace lived in the British Crown Colony of Hong Kong, it was probably safer for Aunt Mary to correspond with me through her.

We knew that my letters would be inspected. But nearly everyone on my campus corresponded with friends and relatives in foreign countries, and using my school address was probably the prudent thing to do.

Her letter was delivered to my school dorm. My English/Chinese mailing label worked. "Now this is more like it!" Aunt Mary wrote back. "Hearing from you is not only a joy, it also keeps me from worrying about you. How about writing one letter a month directly to each other?"

In one of my letters, I wrote, "I now know some 2,000 Chinese characters and can read newspapers, magazines and books."

Aunt Mary responded, "I was delighted to hear about your school activities. Wouldn't Mr. Spears (remember him?) be a whiz and have fun in a class like the one in Newspaper Reading?"

My father grinned when he read the letter. "This line's for me," he said.

I picked up Aunt Mary's letter and read it again. "What makes you think so?"

He laughed. "It's called 'reading between the lines.' Some day you will learn."

I was careful to leave out anything to do with current events or politics. My father often corrected my letters and even helped to type them on his old Remington portable. Once, he could not refrain from slipping in a few lines of his own in the form of a postscript:

Mary: I have just finished typing the foregoing letter for Cheng – his ideas, and wordings partly mine. I don't think there is much to add on my part except perhaps a little apology for this ribbon, which, as you can easily see is fast 'fading away' like its owner. I only hope you won't get sore eyes after reading these two pages. At this moment, the three of us are together for the weekend. We have just finished our dinner. And for the past half an hour, Julia has been 'nursing' that 19th century German-made stove of ours – so that the fire won't go out. She certainly has picked up quite a few tricks since she came back!

From across the Pacific half a world away, Aunt Mary replied:

I know about those old stoves . . . we had one on the farm where I grew up . . . stoked it with corn-cobs and they burned out faster than we could carry them to the house . . . or so it seemed to the kids who supplied the fuel during baking periods.

As years went by, it became apparent that writing was more and more difficult for Aunt Mary. Yet she always remembered my birthday:

Now a birthday message for Cheng . . . and applying to any and every house he may live in. Sorry, I cannot name the author.

Bless the four corners of this house,
And be the lintel blest.
And bless the hearth, and bless the board,
And bless each place of rest.
And bless the door that opens wide
To strangers as to kin,

And bless each crystal window pane
that lets the sunlight in.
And bless the rooftree overhead
And every sturdy wall.
The peace of man, the peace of God,
The peace of love on all.

Love, and happy birthday, dear.

It was a wonder that we managed to keep in touch with each other as long as we did in spite of the Cold War. The last letter I received from Aunt Mary was around May 1956. In the following year, I wrote two more letters but never got an answer.

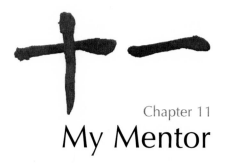

Chapter 11
My Mentor

t the age of fifteen, I was admitted to one of the best all-boys schools in Beijing. It was on the other side of town, and every morning it took me a full hour by bus to get to my new school from my parents' home. As I recall, this was the brief period when I could find Jules Verne in bookstores and libraries, and one was free to choose Li Po over Chairman Mao's poems. It was one of the few moments in my Beijing memory that still stands out with bright colors.

I sat behind Xiao Zhang, a Communist Youth League member who was one of the top students in the class. He was quiet, neat, meticulous and hardworking. His favorite jacket was a hand-me-down from his elder brother who had fought on the Korean battlefield; it was patched over and over at the sleeves, but neatly ironed and spotless.

"I want to study engineering," he told me. His father was a pedicab driver, and Xiao Zhang was the first in the family to enter high school.

One day, Xiao Zhang asked me to help him with the pronunciation of the English letters that were in his algebra and geometry books. He was using Chinese characters to note the phonetics. "M" became "ai moo." I managed to suppress my laughter. The letter X was especially hard for him. Instead of "eks," he pronounced it as "ai kaa si."

For lunch, he often had salted turnips with *woutou*, a steamed bun made from coarse corn flour. In northern China, woutou was regarded as "poor man's food" and hard to digest. But my father told me that it was actually nutritious. One day, my mother steamed a couple of woutou buns. When Zhang saw my lunch, he laughed and said, "Don't get a stomach ache!" He showed me how to toast my steamed buns on a coal stove. They tasted much better, and soon we became good friends.

The following autumn our school went to the countryside to help with the harvest. We took a train part of the way and hiked the rest. The village was located in the remote suburbs of Beijing where there was no electricity for miles and water was drawn from wells. I saw corn grinders made of heavy stones and hauled by draft animals. Piles of sorghum stalks and firewood were stacked against fences and walls. Windows were covered with translucent paper instead of glass panes. I could not believe that I was in such a primitive village in the outskirts of a great capital city. It was like going back to the last century.

The local peasants took us into their homes. I was lodged in Grandma Liu's house with one of my classmates. "Come in, come in," she said with a glowing smile. The place was small but tidy. By the window was an earthen bed covered with bricks and a mat. "That's a *kang*," said the elderly woman. It was heated from underneath with firewood and branches. The kang was hard, but I was dead tired and fell into a deep sleep.

From dawn to dusk we cut and gathered rows and rows of wheat. At first, the work did not seem too hard, and we competed with one another to get in the most rows. By the end of the first day, I could barely stand up, and both of my hands were blistered.

On the third day, I came down with a fever and nasty cough. The Party Secretary of the village came to see me. "Well, well now, young man," he said with a friendly smile, "it looks like we have a little setback here."

I felt ashamed. The old man patted me on my shoulder. "Never mind about the farm work," he said. "Your task now is to get well fast."

Grandma Liu put a cold towel on my forehead and kept the kang nice and warm. She went next door to borrow two fresh eggs from her neighbor. My heart nearly melted when the old woman scooped a handful of millet from a little cloth bag hanging on the wall and cooked a pot of steaming porridge. As I ate the nutritious golden grain, I sensed that she must have been saving it for winter. It was tastier than any other porridge I had eaten.

That night, my fever rose; I shivered and coughed, and began to breathe with difficulty. The curtain opened, and Grandma Liu came in with a lantern. She propped me up with an extra pillow and made me drink a cup of hot water.

There was no doctor in her village. "Don't worry," she said. "We'll get you to Dr. Li's clinic first thing in the morning."

"How far is it from here?" I asked.

"About an hour's ride on a mule cart."

The clinic was a single room partitioned by a curtain. It was a tight space and the walls were turning gray. There was no screen in the doorway; flies flew in and out. But the floor was swept and the waiting space smelled of disinfectants. Dr. Li was wearing a white uniform that was a little tattered but decently clean. There was no running water; he washed his hands in a basin of water with soapsuds floating on the surface. Nonetheless, it was a clinic and the doctor was the only medical provider in the area.

"You must be a city boy." The doctor smiled. He was graying and came across as a gentle and caring person.

I nodded. "I'm here with my school to help with the harvest."

Dr. Li took my temperature and listened through his stethoscope. He thumped my back a couple of times and examined my ears, nose and throat. The diagnosis was bronchitis and asthma. "This is wheat land," he said. "I have patients who come down with asthma at this time of the year." He gave me a shot of streptomycin, a packet of white tablets, and a couple of ephedrine pills for my wheezing.

That evening, my head teacher informed me that I was going home the next day. "But we aren't finished here," I said.

"True," he replied. "But you can't stay here in this condition. We've already made arrangements to take you home."

Early next morning, I found a mule cart waiting in front of the house. Grandma Liu packed some buns for us, handed the driver a thermos of hot water, and covered me with two layers of quilts. The Party Secretary was there to see us off. My favorite physics instructor, Zheng *Laoshi* (teacher) climbed onto the cart and sat across from me. I was glad that he was going with me. Our driver was an old villager, the owner of the mule and cart. Everyone waved and bade us safe journey as our cart started to move.

The old man hummed as he drove us in the direction of the city. A few strands of white clouds floated idly in the pale blue sky. A gentle breeze brushed my face as the mule trotted along the dirt path. We rolled by fields of wheat and barley, and caught glimpses of distant hills painted with autumn-colored maple forests. As I watched the village slowly disappear into the horizon, I wondered if I would ever see it again. I hoped that someday Grandma Liu would enjoy electricity in her home. And I wished Dr. Li would get running water in his examination room.

Towards the afternoon, the old path merged into a wider road, bringing us nearer to urban civilization. Telephone poles and power lines came into view. The thought of electricity flowing into rural villages excited me.

"Many of my classmates want to study electrical engineering and telecommunication," I said.

"Yes," Zheng Laoshi said warmly. "China needs young and educated people like you. You are our future."

"My father says that China needs scientists."

"True!" His face lit up. "Scientists are always at the leading edge of development."

"How come?"

"They study the structure and behavior of the physical and natural world," he replied. "If it weren't for Faraday's experimental work on electromagnetic induction, we would not have electric motors today."

As our mule cart wobbled onwards, I thought about Zheng Laoshi's classes. It occurred to me that he had never instructed his students to "put politics in command" or "be a red expert." Chairman Mao was not in his vocabulary either. Instead, he talked about Galileo and Newton, Faraday and Maxwell, and their quest for science and the truth. It appealed to me as something that was pure and true, and far more admirable and noble than politics.

It happened to be the first anniversary of Sputnik I, humankind's first artificial satellite to be placed into orbit; our class had bubbled with excitement when Zheng explained the significance. Instead of propaganda rhetoric about the great victory of Leninism, he drew parabolic curves and went into the physics of the satellite launch.

"I still remember your talk on the first Sputnik."

"Yes," he said with a thoughtful look.

"You mentioned that if an animal were placed inside the orbiting satellite, it would be weightless. How can that be?"

My teacher found a piece of paper and fumbled in his bag for a pen. "Don't confuse body weight with the body mass," he said. Zheng jotted down some formulas and drew a picture of an orbiting satellite with a monkey on board. Plotting lines, curves and arrows, he explained how the animal lost its support force and entered a sustained state of weightlessness.

"This is what scientists call 'zero gravity.'"

I scratched my head. Somehow I could not grasp zero gravity in an orbiting satellite.

"Sometimes scientists need to use their imaginations," Zheng chuckled. "Imagine yourself in the satellite. Both you and the satellite are actually in a continuous free fall around the earth, but never getting closer to the ground because the earth's surface curves beneath you." A little bulb lit up inside me as I remembered Lewis Carroll's *Alice in Wonderland.* I imagined myself with Alice, falling into the deep rabbit hole without any support force and feeling weightless.

Living in a totalitarian state where there was no freedom of thought, I was tired of listening to lecture after lecture by politically correct instructors who extolled Mao's doctrines and rejected foreign ideas. But here was a young teacher who possessed something else.

That something else was called "the quest for truth and knowledge." I was fascinated.

"May I have the paper you scribbled on?" I inquired.

"This?" He held it up with a smile.

"Yes. I love your diagrams. They remind me of a book I have."

"Can you show it to me someday?"

I hesitated for a moment. "It's published in England."

Zheng Laoshi nodded his head appreciatively and jotted something. "Here's my home address and directions. Come for a visit with your book."

Our cart finally arrived at my home. It was already dark. "Home sweet home," my teacher whispered to me in English.

That night, I went to bed with the happy thought that I had found a mentor.

Chapter 12
The Tiny Circle Grows

The following month, I mustered up my courage to visit Zheng Laoshi's home. "Head west from the bus stop, then turn north when you reach Big Tea Lane, and west at Tobacco Alley." Zheng's instructions read like a mariner's navigation chart, but after half an hour wandering through a labyrinth of winding and crisscrossing alleys and lanes, I lost all sense of direction. Fortunately, I stumbled upon Little Horn Alley, the landmark Zheng had given me to lead me to his house. "It's the smallest alley in town," he said. It was barely wide enough to allow one person through at a time, and a bicyclist had to get off and inch his way sideways.

I must have stared at the solid wooden gate for a good thirty seconds before I was finally convinced that it was the address in Zheng's hand-written directions. I had envisioned my mentor living in a fashionable residence. Instead, before me was a weathered gate in a gray brick wall which looked as though it had suffered a bad beating from Beijing's wintry storms.

I found a rusty bell-shaped piece of metal fastened to the gate. A clapper dangled from the apex. It was a knocker. I tried it a couple of times. Soon, I heard a muffled voice and shuffling sounds. The door creaked on its hinges to reveal an elderly man with a saintly face. He was white-haired and slightly stooped, but his cheeks were rosy and he looked robust. I introduced myself and asked if this was the home of Zheng Laoshi. The old man's lips parted in a warm smile.

"You have found the right house," he replied in perfect English. "I am his father. Did you have difficulty finding our address?" The old man laughed when he saw the surprised look on my face. "I learned English a long time ago – way before you were born."

They lived in a four-room house, small but cozy. A well polished piano with shiny white keys stood upright against the wall of the living room. Beside the piano, a violin and a handsome accordion. I was in a house of music lovers. They all played the piano. One of Zheng's brothers was the top accordion player in the school district, and the other was learning the violin. Now I understood why Zheng's lecture on the physics of sound waves, resonance, timbre and overtones was so vivid.

In my teacher's room, my eyes immediately fell on a wall-to-wall bookshelf filled with scientific books in English, Russian and

Japanese. "Learning a foreign language is like growing another eye," Zheng smiled. "Now, did you say you had some books to show me?"

I unzipped my school bag and pulled out two books. The first one was an old physics textbook in English that my father's friend had found for me. The cover was brown and musty, and the pages were yellow and fragile. Opening to the chapter on light propagation, Zheng Laoshi tossed his head backwards in a roaring laughter. "Ether is an old theory prior to modern physics," he explained. "You really need something more current."

I handed him the other book. It was M. Nelson's *Principles of Physics*, reprinted in 1958. "Now this is more like it," Zheng said with enthusiasm. He studied the table of contents and flipped through the pages. "The exercises look interesting. You ought to study the chapter on photometry; we didn't have a good discussion of this subject in class." Zheng liked the section on electrical energy. "How did you come by this book?"

"From my mother's sister in Hong Kong."

"It's really wonderful that you are keeping up with your English."

"My father says English is an important tool for science and technology."

"Your father is right." Motioning me over to his desk, Zheng pointed to a pile of foreign books and journals. They were all about biological cells and genetics. As early as 1953, he had been following the work of Watson and Crick, and he was also interested in the effect of radiation on genes. I could feel his excitement.

"Take a look at these photographs of my experiments." Zheng opened a photo album of several rows of malformed corn. Each stalk had an amazing multitude of ears of all sizes and descriptions.

I was astonished. He laughed. "They are not for dinner!"

"Gosh, how did you do it? Some kind of fertilizer?"

"Nope, nothing to do with fertilizers or chemicals," he grinned. "I had the seeds exposed to x-ray radiation in a clinic, and planted them in a small plot of land behind my cousin's house. What you see are deformed corn plants. They grew out of the seeds exposed to x-rays."

"Amazing!" I exclaimed.

"I am planning another experiment with ultra-short wave. Would you like to help me?"

"I'd love to!" I said, and agreed to help assemble the equipment.

Our friendship continued to grow over the years. Zheng Laoshi taught me radio electronics and higher math, and I helped him assemble equipment for his experiments. Once, I asked Zheng Laoshi if it was true that he was a religious believer. Taken aback, he asked, "Didn't you know that we're Catholics?"

I paused. "I didn't know which church, but I knew you were Christians."

"Really! How did you know?"

"Your father wished me Merry Christmas last December. And he said in English, 'May the Lord be with you.'"

My mentor laughed. "Yes, that's him all right. He's an active church member, always spreading the gospel. Fortunately, the police haven't caught him in the act."

"I know that you are a committed scientist," I said. "And your research is on the material world. Yet your beliefs are spiritual. Aren't these contradictory?"

Zheng Laoshi drew a large circle about the size of the paper.

"Imagine this as the Universe – a boundless universe of the unknown."
With a sharp pencil, he drew a tiny circle about the size of a dot
inside the Universe. "And this is our knowledge – the sum of what
mankind knows about the Universe. As we learn more about it day
by day, the tiny circle grows. But the more we know, the more we
realize what we do not know. That is the wonder of God's creation.
God encourages us to explore and discover His infinite greatness."

Chapter 13
Rude Awakening

he Voice of America was high on the Chinese government's list of enemy radio stations. It was always jammed; the newscasts were blotted out by constant interference of buzzing frequencies. Luckily, it was not my top choice. If I were to be caught red-handed, my crime would be listening to the Far East Network of the American Armed Forces Radio Service (AFRS) broadcast from Okinawa. I had learned to wind my own shortwave coil and install an eight-tube four-band receiver that could pinpoint *Fibber McGee and Molly, The Lone Ranger*, *Dragnet* and other radio shows I used to enjoy in New York. Once, listening to Jack Benny, I convulsed with laughter until tears came down my cheeks.

"Hush!" cautioned my mother. "Our neighbors will know you're listening to shortwave."

"Impossible," I said, pointing to my headphones.

"Even so," she replied. "Your laughter will give you away."

"How come?"

"People don't laugh like that nowadays. Your laughter sounds too natural and too bourgeois."

We both cracked up.

As a matter of fact, my mother was just as guilty. At Christmas, she would put on my headphones and sing "White Christmas" with Bing Crosby. Once, she hummed the "Marines' Hymn." When I tried to stop her, she argued, "No one around here knows this tune. It even has a revolutionary ring to it."

I do not remember what had prompted me to join the Young Pioneers in 1955. I was fourteen and probably figured it was the forward thing to do. When my father saw my red scarf, he said nothing. He had always been nonpartisan, and his silence was an implicit statement of disappointment which I failed to understand until thirty years after he had passed on.

But I became disillusioned when our political counselor questioned me about my father. "Your father is from the old society," he advised. "You belong to the new society and need to draw the line."

I quit the Young Pioneers soon after.

In senior high, Communist Youth League recruiters tried to

enlist me. I flatly refused. This was my first political mistake, as I learned from my chemistry instructor, who invited me into her office one chilly morning.

Lowering her voice, she said, "I overheard complaints about your lack of interest in political activities. Is it true that you refused to join the Communist Youth League?"

I nodded my head.

She was one of the few elderly instructors who was not a party member. I always respected her honesty and integrity.

"Careful," she warned. "You may not realize it, but you are highly vulnerable, especially because you are from the United States, not to mention that your father worked for the old government. Did you know that your political behavior is recorded in your dossier?"

At first, I could not believe it. It had never occurred to me that refusal to join the Communist Youth League would be construed as bad political behavior. But when her words started to sink in, my body went numb and my chest tightened.

"You and I are just tiny and insignificant bugs," she whispered. "Bugs get squashed if they aren't careful. You may be a top student, and you may have lofty aspirations, but the rest of the world could not care less about a crushed bug."

For many days I could not get the words "crushed bug" out of my mind. I loathed the system of controlling people's minds. I detested politics and avoided politically correct activists. I craved freedom of thought, and more than ever I wanted to leave China.

That weekend, my father and I had a frank discussion about my desire to return to the States. He had suffered with heart problems for many years, and he must have thought about what would happen to my mother and me if he were no longer with us.

"I have no doubt that you would be successful in your pursuit of education in the States," he said. "And you would likely find life more comfortable there. But China is on the rise. I believe that there is a future for you here." Yet deep down my father must have known that someday I was bound to leave.

"Your birth certificate is proof that you were born in New York," he said. "But it isn't your passport back to the States."

"What do you mean?" I asked.

"There are three things you must remember," he said, sounding like a professor. "The American Consulate is bound to ask you why you failed to reclaim your citizenship before you reached twenty-one."

"How could I? All foreign embassies are guarded by Chinese Public Security."

"Precisely. You couldn't contact any foreign representatives without jeopardizing yourself and the family. Your next obstacle is to prove your identity."

He held up my birth certificate. "See this line? 'Place of Birth: Medical Arts Centre Hospital, Borough: Manhattan.' That's where you can get your baby footprints for identification."

"And the third?"

"There is always the chance that the American representative will say that you aren't a U.S. citizen because your father was a Chinese diplomat at the time you were born."

"That's a tough one."

"Just say that you were born outside the Chinese diplomatic quarters."

We had a wall map of the world. "There are three giants in the world," my father continued. Running his finger along the borderline between China and the Soviet Union, he said, "These two giants share a long common border scarred by historical conflicts. They are bound to quarrel and even come to blows someday. That is when relations with the third giant will change."

"You make it sound like *Romance of the Three Kingdoms*," I said.

He smiled. "Although China and the United States do not recognize each other today, they are so big that they cannot fail to see each other. Sooner or later, they are bound to talk to one another. I do not know when it will happen, but when that day comes, you may have an opportunity to go back."

The "Hundred Flowers Campaign" of the mid-Fifties was an unfortunate political movement for many. The name was from a poem that said something like "Let a hundred flowers blossom; let a hundred schools of thought contend." Intellectuals were led to believe that their open and candid opinions would be welcomed. But it was a clever trap.

One evening, my father came home with a frown on his face. "I was reading a poster when I felt a gentle tug at my coat sleeve," he mumbled. "It was my old friend and colleague Lao Min. I was just about to greet him when he raised his eyebrow and whispered, 'Follow me.'" It was like a scene out of a Hitchcock movie. I was naturally intrigued.

"Once we were out of everyone's earshot, he said, 'When you

read the posters, you are bound to feel indignant. When you feel indignant, you are bound to write a poster. And when you write a poster, you are bound to get into trouble.'"

It was no secret that hundreds of thousands of people were put to death in the early 1950s during a campaign against counter-revolutionaries. Nationalist sympathizers and criminals were dragged before mass "trials" and summarily executed.

"You'd better listen to Lao Min," admonished my mother with a worried look.

My father was an outspoken man and never hesitated to criticize the corruption and nepotism he had witnessed while serving the Chinese Nationalist Consulate in New York City.

"Don't worry," he said, "I have never been against the Communists, and I think they know it."

My mother shook her head. "But do you know that we are being watched?"

"Impossible! How could that be?"

"Hush . . . lower your voice," she whispered and motioned us into the inner bedroom. "This morning, Zhang Dasao told me something I couldn't believe at first." We had hired Zhang Dasao to do our heavy laundry. She was a good-natured woman in the neighborhood and got on very well with my mother.

"Last month, the local police station made her report on us."

"You mean spy on us?" asked my father incredulously.

"I don't think she is capable of spying. But they wanted to know who visited us, and what sort of reading materials we have in our house."

"I thought Zhang Dasao was illiterate."

A faint smile flickered on my mother's face, but quickly disappeared. "They asked her to report any suspicious conversations."

"Like what?" My father was dumbfounded.

"Like whether Chiang Kai-shek's name was ever mentioned in our household, and whether you or I ever uttered the words *guang fu da lu*."

"You know what," I chimed in, "when I was in prep school, one of the political counselors asked me the same question. Only I didn't understand the four words."

"It means 'recover the mainland,'" whispered my father in English, who was now looking a little green.

Just as Lao Min had predicted, the Hundred Flowers Campaign turned into an ugly Anti-Rightist Movement. One of my father's top students was stigmatized for stating that American workers own cars. Luckily, he was born of a poor peasant family and was spared from exile. But he was branded "rightist" for life, and eight years later he was subjected to public humiliation again during the Cultural Revolution of the 1960s. Thanks to Lao Min's warning, my father survived the Anti-Rightist Movement unscathed. But it was a rude awakening. In his own words: "Now I am beginning to understand the true meaning of the English word intimidation."

Part 2

1966-1972

Chapter 14
Storm

heng Laoshi remained my friend and mentor long after my schooling days. I was in my mid-twenties and ended up teaching English in my father's school. Because I was American-born with "bad political behavior" recorded in my dossier, I was not encouraged to pursue my interest in science or engineering.

In May 1966, seeing ominous signs of a political storm, Zheng and I agreed it would be best to stop seeing each other until the whole thing blew over. But no one had an inkling that the Cultural Revolution would turn into a horrific destruction on a mass scale, shattering the lives of countless individuals and families. We would not be spared.

I was teaching a first-year class when the storm erupted on my campus. At first, I was not accused of anything in meetings or on big character posters. Then, one hot evening, teachers and students were called to a mass meeting, ostensibly to denounce "Capitalist Roader" Li Qiuye, the president of our college.

Red flags quivered in the spotlights. A giant portrait of Dictator Mao hung ominously against the backdrop of a red curtain. Fists rose as the audience chanted, "Long Live Chairman Mao! Down with Capitalist Roader Li Qiuye!" A female Communist Party member stepped on to the podium and started to expose the "crimes" of "monsters and demons," who turned out to be professors and targeted faculty members hired by Li's office. An English language instructor was charged with poisoning the minds of revolutionary students with Hans Christian Andersen's "The Emperor's New Clothes."

Finally, the speaker yelled into the microphone, "How is it that the American-born son of a reactionary Nationalist official was hired to teach our revolutionary students?" The crowd stopped chanting. I was not mentioned by name but it was obvious whom she meant.

"Do you know that he maintains dubious connections with foreigners? And do you know that he wants to leave the country?" Pounding her fist on the rostrum, the young fanatic howled angrily. "How dare he teach our revolutionary students! Who is responsible for hiring him?!" Raising her fist and screaming at the top of her lungs, she led the crowd in another hysterical round of slogans:

Down with Capitalist Roader Li Qiuye!
Down with monsters and demons!
Long live Chairman Mao!
Long, long live Chairman Mao!

That night, I tossed and turned in my bed with nightmares of red flags, raised fists and cries for blood.

Two days later, I was summoned to the Personnel Director's office. A short, stocky man with a crew cut glared at me from behind a large desk. He was wearing an old army jacket. "Let's see your work identification," he began. I took out my ID and handed it to him. He thrust it into a drawer. "Your contract has expired," he said. "As of today you're no longer in our employment."

I was stunned. "What . . . what contract?"

To my utter amazement, the director said, "You were hired as a contract worker."

"How could it be?!" I exclaimed. "You know very well that I was transferred here from another school."

"Your contract has expired," he repeated.

"Then show me the contract!" I demanded.

The man wavered momentarily, his eyes darting back and forth, avoiding mine. He sneered and said, "Your employment is terminated at the overwhelming request of the revolutionary masses."

"Not true," I countered. "No one has called for my resignation or termination. Why am I being laid off?"

"This is not a capitalist society," he said in a low rasping voice. "We don't lay off people in Socialist China."

"Since this is Socialist China, where did the 'contract' come from?" I could feel my blood boiling.

He hesitated and turned red in the face. "You are no longer employed here. You are now an unemployed street youth," he said, ignoring my question. The word "contract" disappeared from his vocabulary. "Go to your neighborhood police station and ask them to find work for you."

I knew that he was lying through his teeth. I also knew that there was a hiring freeze nationwide. The only work he was referring to was on a farm in some remote rural area.

I had no choice but to leave. On my way out, I tried to visit the Director of the English Language Department. She had fallen under attack and declined to discuss the matter with me. It was not until much later that I realized that I had become an embarrassing piece of baggage that had to be gotten rid of.

Desperately, I sought help from several organizations. At the Commission for Overseas Chinese Affairs, one of the cadres exclaimed, "You, a contract worker? What sheer nonsense!" Even the neighborhood police station was baffled by my situation; the officer simply said, "You aren't a street youth. We don't have your personnel record. Your work unit has it, and they should be fully responsible."

I went back to my school and confronted the Personnel Director about my file.

"File? I have no idea where it is." With an innocent look on his face, he said no more. Behind him sat the young cadre who was originally responsible for transferring me from another school. I glanced at him. But the young man kept quiet and avoided my gaze. I was getting nowhere. I was green at this, and I knew that the director was putting me on.

"It's no use fighting them," my father sighed when I got home. His face wrinkled in sadness. "File or no file, the whole thing is immaterial now."

"What do you mean?"

"The whole country is sucked into a political hurricane. Everyone's future is at stake."

"But I am out of a job!"

"I am sorry, my son. But I fear that the barometer is falling even further."

Ominous dark clouds had already begun to loom on the horizon as extremists had begun to assemble Red Guard organizations. "It doesn't look good," my father said.

"Are you saying I can't do anything about my unemployment?"

"I'm afraid not. We're all in for a long train ride with no stops before the end. No one knows where or when it will arrive at its final destination. So you may as well settle down on the train."

Sure enough, on August 18, 1966, a million Red Guards assembled at Beijing's huge Tiananmen Square. At dawn, the "Great Leader, Great Helmsman" Chairman Mao appeared to a frenzied welcome and mingled with the delirious Red Guards for several hours. A schoolgirl pinned a Red Guard armband on him while the crowd chanted, "Long live our supreme commander Chairman Mao!" It was almost like a scene out of Hitler's fanatical gathering of Brown Shirts.

Soon, Red Guards hit the streets with demonstrations against "monsters and demons," triggering a nationwide rampage. They destroyed antiques and ancient art, defaced statues of Buddha, hacked to pieces the Statue of Liberty overlooking Sun Yat-sen

Memorial Hall in Guangzhou (Canton), and painted over priceless carvings and paintings in the Summer Palace of Beijing. "Landlords" and "capitalists" were rounded up and thrown into kangaroo courts. Anyone who had Western friends, books, or clothing was subjected to persecution. Homes were ransacked. Books were set on fire.

For five years I was unemployed. Meanwhile, Li Qiuye, our college president, committed suicide and the campus became a combat arena of competing Red Guard factions. During the first two chaotic years, the Red Guards were preoccupied with factional fighting and my ailing father was left to his medical leave at home.

Being unemployed was humiliating and painful for me. The only good thing that came out of it was the time I got to spend with my father.

My father had translated literary works for the Foreign Languages Press. Among the notable works he rendered into English were Tian Han's *Wencheng Gongzhu* and *Guan Hanqing*, and Guo Moruo's *Cai Wenji*. One year, he translated Fidel Castro's speech from Spanish into English. On weekends, he spent hours imparting his knowledge to me. "Just teaching my son the tricks of the trade," he would tell his friends with a grin. He taught me how to translate news articles, commentaries, and banquet speeches from Chinese into English. Now and then, he would come up with a difficult sentence or phrase for me to translate on the spot. Sometimes he would challenge me to find a better expression. He was constantly after idiomatic language and strove to understand the author's original meaning.

One day, he cut out a news article from the *People's Daily* and said, "Want to translate this into English?" But I was feeling depressed about my predicament and lost interest in everything.

"You're lucky Father is around to teach you," my mother said. "Stop feeling sorry for yourself and take advantage of this opportunity to practice your translation skills."

I had to admit that she was right. I reached for the Chinese news article and set to work.

My unemployment turned out to be anything but uneventful. A work team was sent to our neighborhood to mobilize the masses (retirees and unemployed people, including housewives) to expose hidden enemies of the Party. The Cultural Revolution was actually a power struggle within the upper echelons of the Communist Party. But this and other kinds of intimidation were used to keep the common people subdued while the country was in chaos.

The image of my mother sitting on a small wooden stool in a dimly-lit meeting hall lingers in my memory to this day. She often sat next to Grandma Song, our 80-year-old neighbor, while the work team lectured the crowd. "If you remember any suspicious happenings," cried the team leader, "reveal now. If you've done anything wrong, confess now."

"I wasn't really scared," she told me afterwards. "What have I to be afraid of?"

"Exactly," I said.

"We have nothing to conceal or reveal."

"You know, as I sat there, I actually dreamed of the ship we were on when we left the Philippines in 1949."

"Daydreaming at a revolutionary meeting is an offense," I joked. "Don't let them catch you."

But I remembered the ship. It was a Swedish freighter bound for San Francisco with six passengers on board. My mother was the only woman. At dinnertime, the captain and the men would wait for her. The moment we entered the room, all rose, and the captain assisted my mother to her place next to him at the dining table covered with white cloth, sparkling plates, glasses and silver utensils. My mother, dressed in a high-collared Chinese silk gown, jade earrings and high-heeled shoes, looked radiant and beautiful.

"And here I am," reflected my mother, "old, useless, hunched in a dark hall like a criminal suspect. How humiliating!"

I was drafted by the Neighborhood Committee to dig air raid tunnels in the backyard. The head of the Committee resembled a gorilla and weighed at least 200 pounds. She was the master informant, and all spies in our neighborhood reported to her. She routinely inspected backyards and hallways, taking notes on anything that looked fishy. My mother nicknamed her Madame Defarge, after the vengeful villain of *A Tale of Two Cities*. Every day, she rounded up all the conscripts for the tunnel project. She would stride into our backyard and holler my name. Sometimes, she charged right into our apartment without knocking and marched me downstairs to the tunnel.

I teamed up with Xiao Ma, a young Chinese Muslim. He was just out of high school and would have been sent to the countryside to work had it not been for his poor health. Xiao Ma was a cheerful individual; he often cracked jokes and sang while we worked. We actually had fun mixing mud and clay with our bare feet and helping old Colonel Ye fire adobe bricks.

"Do you remember my hometown?" my mother asked me one evening.

"Yes, but very little," I said. "Were you daydreaming again?"

She nodded. "Gulangyu, Drum Waves Island." It was a small island off the coast of Amoy. "I miss the beach," she said wistfully. "The sand was so white and fine."

"I remember Big Uncle took me there on a fishing expedition," I said. "We came back empty handed though." My mother chuckled.

Most of the local inhabitants knew her family. Her great grandfather had owned a business, a bank and even a dock. But her grandfather lost nearly everything to bankruptcy when she was a student in Shanghai. When she and I visited her family in 1947 on our way to the Philippines, they were residing in a two-story building on the island. Downstairs, there was a lovely little garden of flowers and vegetables.

"When I was a child, my sisters, brothers, cousins and I would parade around the garden with paper lanterns on Chinese New Year's Eve," my mother said. "Luckily your great, great grandfather isn't alive today. He would surely be a class enemy."

Chapter 15
Persecution

One summer day in 1968, I was remarking to my mother how strangely quiet the neighborhood was when a pack of bullies wearing red armbands led by a tall, dark young man burst into our apartment.

"Tsung Wei-hsien, come out!" he bellowed at the top of his lungs. My father, face white but unfazed, came out of the bedroom. "You're a spy for the American imperialists!" With these words, the leader held up a mock warrant, and two ruffians seized my father's arms.

"I have heart disease and cannot possibly run away," my father said with composure. "May I put on my jacket first?"

The leader blinked. The two let go of my father and followed him into the bedroom. More people came in, among them colleagues from the English Language Department who pretended not to know me. The local policeman and a handful of Neighborhood Committee members also showed up.

As my father was led out, he cast a quick glance at me. I felt a tight knot in my stomach at the dreadful thought that we would never see him again.

My mother and I watched helplessly as the Red Guards ransacked our home, dumping the contents of every drawer, suitcase and box onto the floor, and combing through every piece of clothing, books, notebooks and what few photographs we had left. One of them even went through our cookie jars and biscuit boxes, and scattered my mother's sewing kit.

Suddenly, everyone stopped and gathered around a small writing desk beside my bed. "Is this yours?" asked the leader, pointing to my amateur radio set, which I had unwittingly placed inside the desk. A headphone was plugged to the receiver, which was installed on an aluminum chassis with no cover, exposing a large transformer and eight conspicuous electronic vacuum tubes.

The leader whipped out a notebook and began to cross-examine me. It soon became evident that neither he nor his pack of followers knew much about radios. He whispered something into the ear of one of his henchmen, who dashed out of the room and came back with a man who turned out to be an electrician. The man examined the radio circuit and asked me a couple of knowledgeable questions. His face said it all; my radio set was not capable of transmitting cryptic signals. To my relief, he made no mention of the inductance coil. Tuning in to foreign stations was a crime, and the thick silver coil for shortwave reception was a dead giveaway.

"What's this?" asked one of the thugs, pointing to a large photograph of me and my sixth-grade classmates.

"My graduation picture," I said. "I went to a public school in New York."

"Who's this?" He pointed to a Caucasian man with a mustache, who probably resembled a CIA agent.

"School principal," I answered.

By the time the Cultural Revolution first broke out, we had already shredded and burned nearly all of our English books, letters and photographs. Even my mother's Social Security card and my father's Columbia University papers were set to flame in the coal stove. But we saw no harm in keeping my grade school photograph.

The gang finally withdrew, leaving my radio. But they took away my school picture.

My mother and I leaned against the wall, speechless and confused. I felt numb all over, but my mother remained calm and collected. "Go and get my slippers," she whispered.

The room was topsy-turvy, except for the slippers, which remained in front of her bed in plain sight. My mother pulled out a sock from her right slipper. She reached inside the sock and slipped out a folded paper. I opened it. To my amazement, it was my New York City birth certificate, wrinkled but intact.

"I thought we had burned everything," I murmured. The corners of her mouth curled into a faint smile, but my mother said nothing.

My mother and I are standing in front of our first home
behind the Drum Tower, Beijing, in a small compound
shared by two other faculty families. The wood board
leaning against the wall was a school-issued bed for my
mother, who found it too hard to sleep on. Luckily, Uncle
Wei gave her a couch-bed, ancient but with genuine springs.

Chapter 16

In God's Care

j ust as suddenly as he had been whisked away, my father was brought home the following night. His face looked deathly pale and his ankles were as thick as his lower limbs. His heart condition had deteriorated considerably, but he was required to report to his school every morning for further questioning.

"We are allowing your father to come home for humanitarian reasons," claimed the escort. In a menacing tone, he added, "You are responsible for him. If he tries to run away or commit suicide, you will be held accountable. Understand?"

My father never mentioned corporal punishment or physical

abuse. When I asked him about his cracked spectacles, all I could get out of him were humorous caricatures of his interrogators.

"Did they put you through struggle meetings?" I asked.

He shrugged and replied, "When the crowd shouted, 'Down with Liu Shaoqi! Down with Tsung Wei-hsien!' I actually felt honored to be put on the same level as Chief of State Liu."

The Purge Class Enemy Team interrogated my father about the Hoover Research Institute at Stanford University where he had worked briefly in the early 1950s. His "crimes" consisted of translating mainland Chinese local newspapers and periodicals into English. Actually, my father had already covered all of this in his biographical report when he first arrived in Beijing in 1953; he did not attempt to hide anything from the Communist authorities. But the persecutors alleged that the United States Air Force and Central Intelligence Agency had used my father's translations for determining bombing targets in mainland China. One of the interrogators tried to coerce my father into admitting that he was sent by the director of the Hoover Institution to spy on China.

Somehow, my father hung in there and doggedly insisted that he had returned to China only because he loved his country. "I was really hurt," he told me, "when one of the interrogators banged his fist on the table and called me a 'dog spy.' But I reminded myself that if this were truly an espionage case, why had not the Public Security police come for me instead?"

The winter of 1969 was especially harsh. It was the fourth year into Mao's Cultural Revolution. The cold wind from the north howled with rage. My mother and I had just finished dinner when there was a knock on the door.

It was our neighbor, Mr. Hu. He was Shanghainese, always well-groomed and courteous. He was a Communist Party member but with a touch of bourgeois charm about him. Without a doubt, he was from a well-off family. For the most part, he had survived the Cultural Revolution pretty much unscathed, although there were a couple of posters criticizing him for his bourgeois tastes and habits.

"Is your father in?" Mr. Hu inquired.

"Resting in there," I answered, pointing to our bedroom.

"I need to have a word with him now."

I led him to my father's bedside. Mr. Hu paused; his face reddened. "I apologize for waking you up," he said to my father. "But I'm here to advise you to return to the interrogation room first thing on Monday morning."

"But look at his ankles," I said. I lifted the quilt. My father's ankles were swollen from congestive heart failure. "How can he? He's coughing out a lot of white foam."

"I am sorry, Comrade Tsung," Mr. Hu said, looking perturbed. "Those were orders from the Revolutionary Committee."

"Thank you, Lao Hu," my father interposed. "I will try to be there on time."

I never understood why my father called him "Lao Hu," which was customarily an informal way of addressing old friends and colleagues. Perhaps this was my father's subtle way of letting Hu know that he understood the man's situation. Looking visibly relieved, Mr. Hu bowed slightly and withdrew.

"How can you go there in this condition?!" my mother exclaimed.

"I'll be all right," he smiled. "Did you notice that this time only one person came to get me instead of a legion of Red Guards? This may be a sign of improvement." He still had his sense of humor. But we all knew perfectly well that my father was just putting up a brave front to comfort my mother. There was no alternative but for him to go.

My father coughed again, breathing heavily and spitting out white foam. "I have no regrets for myself," he said. "It was my own choice to return to my homeland . . . "

I held his hand. My eyes blurred, and I felt a warm tear roll down my cheek. "But your mother doesn't deserve this," he continued, gasping for air. "And you've lost your job on account of me . . . I am truly sorry . . . "

I tried to say something, but he raised his hand. "Promise to take good care of your mother." I nodded, and vowed that I would take care of her for the rest of her life.

"You will be okay," I said.

He shook his head. "If anything happens, contact your mother's family. They're the only ones you can depend on for help."

I started to apologize for the years I had blamed my father for bringing us to mainland China. But he shook his head and said, "Your promise is all that matters to me now. Be strong."

Suddenly, my father started to cough out pink foam. "Quick! Get some help," my mother cried out.

We had lost contact with nearly all of our acquaintances, and most of our neighbors had been avoiding us. Who would dare to come to our aid? Out of desperation, I stole across the hallway and knocked on the door of Mr. Yu, an old friend and colleague who used to work with my father in the French Language Department.

I still remember the surprise and compassion on Mr. Yu's kind face when he opened the door. This was a time when colleagues, neighbors, friends and even family members turned against each other for survival. But here was a man who did not hesitate to come to our aid.

"This is serious," Yu said when he saw my father. "I'll get Comrade Hu." Yu was not a Party member, so Mr. Hu's presence was needed.

"Phone for a taxi," instructed the Party man.

The taxi arrived. Slowly and painfully, Mr. Yu and I assisted my father out of bed. My father was tall and difficult to carry. We lived on the second floor and there was no elevator. I wondered how we were going to make it. But there was no time. We proceeded slowly out of our apartment, inched our way along the corridor and carefully down the stairs to the ground level. By then, several neighbors were roused by the noise and came out to witness the event. It seemed to take forever, but we eventually made it to the front entrance of the building.

I opened the door. A gust of freezing air burst in. My father coughed and gasped for breath as we huddled at the building entrance.

The taxi was parked at a distance from where we stood. My father suddenly lost consciousness. The driver saw us, but made no attempt to move closer. Just then, I heard a loud and commanding voice from behind us: "Drive over here now!"

We got my father into the car. Someone helped my mother into the front seat. I sat in the rear with my father's head in my lap.

"To the nearest ER," ordered Mr. Hu and closed the door. We were on our way.

"How is he?" my mother asked.

"Unconscious," I said. "Don't worry. We're almost there."

But I knew that my father was already dead. I closed his eyelids with the palm of my right hand and cradled him in my arms.

When we arrived, the driver jumped out of the car and sprinted inside. Two men in white ran out with a gurney and rushed him to the emergency room where the doctors tried to revive him with injection and resuscitation.

Eventually, one of the doctors came to me and shook his head. My mother broke down sobbing. I felt like crying myself. But I remembered my father's last words.

I signed some papers and was told to return to the hospital at 8:00 the following morning for final arrangements. A hospital aide wheeled my father's body out of the emergency room. My mother and I followed him through a long dark corridor into a small room that was poorly lit and very cold.

My mother sobbed and refused to leave. Eventually, I persuaded her to go home with me.

We made it home in a pedicab and went straight to our bedroom. As I was tucking my mother into her bed, I heard the door open. In slipped Grandma Song and her daughter, whose husband was a professor and had also fallen victim to the Red Guards. Grandma Song put her finger to her lips and stealthily closed the door behind them. The two approached my mother, who was too weak to get up.

I told them everything about my father's ordeal. Grandma Song's daughter looked at her in disbelief. But the old woman nodded her head. She had fled to the inland city of Chongqing during the Japanese invasion and lived through civil wars. She had experienced hardship and fear, witnessed the cruelty of war and human suffering. But her kind face always shone with hope, compassion and faith.

"You must let him go," she whispered and stroked my mother's forehead. "Lao Tsung was a good person. He was an honest man. He is now in Heaven, in God's care." She turned to me. "Perhaps it is better this way, for he no longer has to suffer. The place where they will cremate your father's body is way up north and extremely cold. Your mother is ill; she won't make it there. Let them return his ashes to earth. We can take comfort in knowing that his soul is now in Heaven."

They stayed for a few more minutes. "It is dark times," Grandma Song whispered to me when I saw them to the door. "But tomorrow is a new day. When a cart arrives at the foot of a mountain, there must be a way across."

I opened our door and peeked into the corridor to see if it was safe for them to leave. No one was there.

I could not sleep most of the night. Only a few hours before, my father was still alive. Now his bed was empty. I took consolation in the knowledge that at least my father died in my arms instead of alone in a detention room.

I was not a religious person. But I always knew that my mother came from a Christian family. She often prayed, even though we were in a Communist state where Christianity was banned. Grandma Song's words had an immediate effect on her. Perhaps there was some truth in *linghun* (soul) and God after all.

It comforted me. I was ready for tomorrow.

A small light bulb dangled from the high ceiling and barely lit the chilly hospital room. I assisted my mother to a chair where she sat staring at the lifeless body of my father. Her eyes were dry; she had no more tears to shed.

There were two strangers in the room, one wearing military green and the other in a dark blue Mao jacket with a red band on his arm. A portrait of Mao Zedong was mounted on the rear wall with a placard bearing his famous quotation: "After the enemies with guns have been wiped out, there will be enemies without guns." I showed them the Zhongshan tunic suit we had brought for my father. The army man nodded. The other grunted and said, "Make it quick."

I peeled the tattered nightclothes off my father and proceeded to put on the clean shirt and suit. His body seemed heavier and his limbs were stiff. I struggled with the sleeves and tugged at the trouser legs. No one lifted a finger to help. I never imagined that I would someday be handling a dead body, let alone my father's. But it was the only thing that I could do for him. The words "rise to the occasion" came to my mind. It was one of my father's favorite English expressions. For a split second, I thought I saw a smile on his face. My father was now free of wrinkles and looked at peace.

I took out a comb and was about to straighten his hair when my mother said, "Let me do it." The two men stared at her like robots.

She combed his hair, knelt down and kissed his cheek. I went down on my knees beside her. In a serene voice audible only to us, my mother whispered, "*Tian bao you.* God bless and protect you."

"What about this?" asked the man in blue, pointing to my

father's eyeglasses on the table next to the pile of old clothes.

"We'll keep the glasses," I answered.

"Then sign your name here." He opened the door while I scrawled my signature on a form. Two burly men came into the room with a gurney. "Let's get on with it," he ordered. My mother and I watched them cover up my father. We followed them to a truck that was waiting outside the building. They loaded the body onto the vehicle. The driver fired up the engine and drove towards the hospital gate.

Arm in arm, my mother and I stood at the building entrance. No funeral, no burial. Just two loved ones bidding farewell. We watched the truck drive through the gate, make its way into the streets, and recede further and further into the distance until we could see it no more.

I took out my father's glasses. I could almost see his intelligent eyes and humorous smile. The frame had cracked below both lenses, and one of the earpieces was glued and taped together. When I had asked him about it, he would not say anything about the kangaroo court. Instead, he mumbled something about a clumsy fall. I pocketed the spectacles. I knew if my father were still alive, he would have wanted me to move on.

"Farewell," I whispered, and vowed not to turn back.

The north wind stopped howling when my mother and I got home from the hospital. We were in mourning and needed a moment of peace and time to reflect. I stood by the window, gazing at the gray clouds drifting into the distance. In the eyes of the State, my father had died in disgrace. I was out of a job, and I worried about my ailing mother. We were just two tiny leaves in the storm, lost in the land of chaos.

My father's belongings were scattered all over the bedroom. I was removing his soiled clothes and tidying up his bed when I came across a notebook with a plastic red cover. To my surprise, names, dates and places in English and Chinese filled page after page in his shaky cursive handwriting.

"A diary?" I whispered to my mother.

She shook her head. "It could be his 'confessions.'"

As I flipped through the pages, I recalled what my father told me shortly after his release from detention. He'd had a talent for creating caricatures with words, and many of his stories hid his disappointments and misgivings with humor. He had described how he was led into a room full of old professors and intellectuals who were writing their "confessions" under the watchful eyes of "a midget with a small mustache" he referred to as "Little Mustache." Little Mustache had ordered my father to confess, his upper lip twitching like Charlie Chaplin's imitation of Adolph Hitler. But my father was innocent and would not fabricate a story. So he had written truthful accounts of his past.

I read my father's journal and memorized parts of it. "Careful," my mother cautioned. "They may come for it."

Three days later, two ruthless-looking men came to our apartment and demanded the notebook. One of them asked, "Did you read it?

He was a diminutive figure with a twitching mustache.

"No," I lied and gave them the journal.

This is the last photograph of my father, taken a year before the Cultural Revolution. The typewriter behind him was an old Remington portable.

Chapter 17
Dawn

t first, I did not recognize the significance of the Chinese-Russian skirmishes over a tiny island on the northeast border in early 1969. But the clashes soon escalated and the Soviets became China's top enemy, while the Chinese were secretly making up with the Americans. I had no inkling that Beijing and Washington had begun to exchange messages through French President Charles de Gaulle, American journalist Edgar Snow and other notables. Premier Zhou Enlai, a well-respected pragmatist and statesman, had returned to center stage; the political landscape at home was starting to shift. Even the atmosphere in our building was improving.

Neighbors began to greet us in the hallway and struck up small conversations. Grandma Song and a couple of old acquaintances started to visit my mother openly.

In mid-April that year, I got my first break in the form of a piece of paper that was of no monetary value, but infinitely priceless. It was a Revolutionary Worker Death Certificate that recognized my father's 1953 repatriation as a patriotic action.

"We are genuinely grieved by Lao Tsung's death," said Comrade Xu, who handed it to me. Xu was the new director of our school faculty. Two others were present. All three were top graduates and former students of my father.

"What I am trying to say," Xu continued with a broad smile, "is that your father was a patriotic person. Our Party and the Government's policy has always been to welcome compatriots like your father. He had committed a serious mistake, but because he came clean with everything, our policy is to let bygones be bygones."

Relief spread through my body when I suddenly realized that my father's name had been cleared. My hands trembled as I read the document. I could not help feeling how tragic all this had been. My father's death was untimely and needless.

"Poor Father," my mother said as she got into her bed that evening. "He was such a proud man before, and now look what has happened. He died a broken man accused of spying against his own country."

My mother slept on an old, worn-out sofa. It was the only furniture in our apartment that had springs. A small black-and-white photograph of my father stood on a desk. It had escaped the notice of the Red Guards. Nearly all of his pictures were either destroyed or confiscated.

"Did he know that his name would be cleared some day?" I wondered.

"He was innocent and his conscience was clear," said my mother. "Now that his case is closed, may his soul rest in peace." She closed her eyes in prayer.

I sat beside the sofa as my mother nestled in her cotton-padded quilt. A blanket of silence covered the room as we spoke in whispers.

"I wonder what actually happened behind the scenes," she murmured.

"What do you mean?"

"The school still maintains that he committed a 'serious mistake,' and yet the death certificate recognizes his repatriation."

"Must be some higher-up authority," I replied.

"Yes, but who?"

Good question. Our school reported to both the Ministry of Foreign Trade and Ministry of Higher Education. But I doubted if any of them would have any say in his case.

"Don't know. But I'll bet Uncle Wei would know," I said.

Uncle Wei and my father had been classmates in Huiwen Middle School and graduated from Yen Ching University together. They were buddies and my father had often confided in Uncle Wei.

"I'll visit Uncle Wei tomorrow," I said.

"Why the hurry? This may be a bad time for visits."

"We've been isolated too long and I need to get my job back. It's high time to reach out for advice."

"If you must, see his son first."

I considered for a moment. As a member of the younger generation, his son, Xiao Yong, was less likely to be victimized by the political storm. I accepted my mother's prudent advice.

I paced up and down the room as my mother fell asleep. I glanced at the photograph of my father. It was the last picture of him taken just before the Cultural Revolution; he was about fifty-eight years old. His hair was black, except for his sideburns, which had started to gray, and his hairline had begun to recede on the right temple. He was sitting by the desk, his rickety old Remington portable typewriter and favorite books in the background.

I walked over to the desk and felt the books with my fingers, reminiscing about the days when my father used to teach me to read and write. I picked up his favorite *Oxford Concise Dictionary*, a dark blue hardcover book he often humorously referred to as the "best authority" in the house. Next to it was a worn-out *Webster's Dictionary* that must have weighed ten pounds and had traveled here with us from halfway around the world.

An old newspaper clipping protruded from the *Webster*. It was an article about General Li Tsung-jen, former acting president of Nationalist China who left Taiwan and defected to mainland China in 1965. He was greeted at Beijing Airport by Premier Zhou Enlai and one hundred other officials, including a handful of ex-Nationalist officials who had left the Taiwan regime earlier. It was a memorable event, described in the paper as a "resounding victory." Why did my father keep this news clipping?

Something clicked in the back of my mind. But I was not sure. Perhaps Uncle Wei could shed some light.

I got up at the crack of dawn, hopped onto a bus and headed towards the southeastern section of the city, where Uncle Wei and his family still lived. Uncle Wei was a true native of Old Beijing, and he was like a brother to my father. I felt a surge of excitement as I got off the bus, turned into Little South Street and proceeded north.

The walls along the main streets were still covered with big character posters. From what I could tell, there was still some infighting among the Red Guards.

At last, I spotted a familiar alley, but the road sign was different. After circling it a couple of times, I realized that the name must have been changed when the zealous Red Guards were trying to destroy the Four Olds – Old Customs, Old Culture, Old Habits, Old Ideas – including any street name that did not have a revolutionary ring to it.

The heavy gate that had always been left wide open was now locked. Its coat of red paint was starting to fade and peel off. But the hole where Uncle Wei had inserted a braid of firecrackers for the Year of the Horse was still there. I tried the brass knocker. A harsh voice called out from behind. "Who's there?"

I was dressed like a local, my accent was acceptable, and I could pass myself off as a native. "Old schoolmate!" I shouted.

The gate opened with a loud squeak. A woman I didn't recognize appeared in the entrance.

"Who are you?" she asked suspiciously, eyeing me up and down.

Something told me that she was a "red category" person who spied on neighbors and reported to the local police on any "questionable" happenings in the neighborhood.

"Xiao Yong's old schoolmate," I lied.

She led me in and called, "Comrade Wei! An old schoolmate is here to see you." She took my word for it, and I felt like a bona fide undercover agent.

Fortunately it was Yong's wife who came out. She recognized me. Perhaps it was due to her training as a nurse that she was not as excitable as my friend Yong. Without missing a beat, she said, "You're a little late. Yong is expecting you. Come on in."

As I followed her in, I cast a quick glance around the courtyard where we had found temporary lodging many years ago. Laundry lines crisscrossed the length of the compound that was no longer well maintained. The door of the room we once lived in looked intact, but it had a large padlock on it. The old water pump was still in the middle of the courtyard. Pails were scattered on the ground near the pump. There was something different about the place. I sensed that something significant had taken place in the lives of the Wei family. Besides, who was that woman?

Yong must have taken his wife's cue. "Come right on in," he said loud enough for the "red" woman, who pretended to be occupied but was all ears.

Yong closed the door.

"What happened?" I whispered.

"We're all right, but we've lost most of our property." I knew that Uncle Wei's rental properties, farm and two cows had been confiscated during the Communist takeover of Beijing in 1949, and he had been sentenced to "reform through labor," gathering cow dung and cleaning pigsties. And now, sixteen years later, Yong told me, his living quarters were taken away – this time by Cultural Revolutionary fanatics armed with *The Little Red Book of Mao* quotations. The Red Guards had requisitioned the main rooms in the north wing by decree of the revolutionary masses, and illegally appropriated them for one of their own families. And now his family and his parents were crammed into two small rooms on opposite sides of the main quarters.

Thankfully, Uncle Wei had not suffered any physical abuse or detention. There was only one wall poster that denounced his capitalist background and "bourgeois way of life," and he was assigned to relatively light manual chores around the school campus for "reeducation" and "redemption."

Yong led me to his parents' place in the opposite wing.

"Little Cheng!" Uncle Wei greeted me warmly, clasping my hands. Aunty Wei hugged and kissed me, and dabbed her eyes with a handkerchief as she hurried off to prepare tea and pastries.

Uncle Wei was not surprised about my father. "Actually, Lao Tsung had a close encounter with the Public Security police about fifteen years ago," he whispered.

Taking my arm, he led me to the back of the room away from the window. "We can talk more conveniently here." At first, I did not understand what he meant by "conveniently." Then I remembered the expression "walls have ears."

"You probably don't know anything, since you were only eleven or twelve," he began. "When your father first visited me in 1953, I simply said, 'What a fool you are for coming to mainland China!'" He patted me on the shoulder. "Lao Tsung came back for patriotic reasons. His intentions were honest. But as it turned out, he was in deep trouble, and I was the one friend in town he could think of to help him." He paused. "But there was something unusual about his case."

"What do you mean?"

"I'll get to that in a minute. Your father arrived in Beijing with a group of repatriated scholars. They were admitted to the Returned Overseas Chinese Students Guest House. The debriefing and ideological 'education' lasted much longer than he had expected. When you and your mother arrived in Beijing, he started to look for a job on his own. The authorities were upset by this 'extracurricular' activity. When the guest house reported the loss of a radio set, Public Security was brought in and Lao Tsung became a chief suspect."

"Why?"

"He was the only guest who frequently went out for 'extracurricular' activities. He was innocent, of course, but there was no such thing as a court of justice or defense attorney."

Uncle Wei stopped to offer me a cup of tea and help himself to one. Xiao Yong sat by the window spellbound.

"Lao Tsung looked like a ghost when he walked into my home that evening," Uncle Wei reminisced.

"What happened? Was he arrested?"

Uncle Wei smiled and pointed upwards. "Thank Heaven, no. The Public Security found the real culprit. Turned out to be a staff worker of the guest house who stole the radio and hid it under his bed."

"You said that it was an unusual case. What did you mean?"

Uncle Wei leaned forward and replied, "Ordinarily, the Public Security is quick to haul in suspects and could have easily arrested your father, evidence or no evidence. Yet, someone higher up must have kept them from doing so."

"Who?"

"Don't know. Only a hunch. You see, Lao Tsung was a Chinese Nationalist diplomat for more than twenty years in the West, and he returned to our country at a time when the Chinese Communist Government was trying to win over personages like him."

I reached into my pocket for my father's Revolutionary Worker Death Certificate and showed it to Uncle Wei.

He put on his glasses while Aunty Wei poured me another cup of tea and packed a couple of steamed stuffed buns for me to take home to my mother.

Uncle Wei handed back the document and said, "I suspect that your father's repatriation must have something to do with Premier Zhou Enlai."

"How come?" I asked.

"At the time, Premier Zhou was also the Foreign Minister. Your father had been Chinese Nationalist Consul and Consul General. Surely he must have caught the attention of Premier Zhou when he made known his intention to repatriate to the mainland."

"It makes sense," I said. "But how can we be sure?"

"The Revolutionary Worker Death Certificate could not have happened without the approval from higher up, and my guess is it was approved by the Premier's office."

"Then write to the Premier about the job you lost," suggested Xiao Yong.

"It's a long shot," said Uncle Wei. "But worth a try."

It was getting late. As I prepared to leave, Uncle Wei accompanied me to the door and whispered, "The Lord is near. Be patient."

Chapter 18

A Long Shot

he early morning air was pleasantly cool. A soldier patrolled nearby as I alighted from the bus clutching a brown envelope. Guards armed with revolvers and rifles stood at the main entrance of the State Council across the street. A black limousine rolled out; the guards snapped to attention and gave a smart military salute.

I drew a deep breath and stood hesitantly on the opposite sidewalk. For days I had been preparing myself for this moment. I summoned up my courage and proceeded to cross the street in the direction of the huge and imposing main entrance.

My right foot barely touched the road when one of the armed

guards raised his hand and shouted, "Halt!" Another raised his rifle, took a few steps in my direction and yelled, "Stay where you are!"

The soldier on patrol strode over to me and demanded, "What is your business here?"

I instantly retracted my foot, feeling a tight knot in my stomach. The soldier repeated his question. There was a grim look on his face. He wore a large brown holster on his belt.

"I . . . I am trying to deliver this to the Premier's Reception Post," I stammered. I handed him the envelope.

He took it from me and examined it. It was for Premier Zhou Enlai, with my name and return address on it.

"Where are you from?" he asked.

"I live on Peace Lane outside Anding Gate. I'm a repatriated Chinese from overseas."

As I tried to explain the purpose of the letter, the officer interrupted me. "Wait. Did you say you were a Huaqiao?" he asked.

"Yes," I nodded.

"Which country are you from?" he asked in a friendlier tone. By then, the sentries across the street had returned to their positions and resumed their guarding posture.

When I told him that I was from the United States, the soldier's face lit up with a smile. "*Meiguo Huaren*, American Chinese."

I felt a little more at ease now. I explained why I was writing to Premier Zhou's reception post.

"Yes, we have a reception post, but it isn't here." Pointing to the bus stop, he said, "Take that bus and get off four stops from here. That is where Premier Zhou's reception post is."

I thanked him.

"You can't miss it," he added as I started to walk towards the bus stop. "You'll see a large crowd there."

As he said, there was a long column of people lining up in front of a makeshift reception post. They were mostly from out of town. Many had travelers' bags and suitcases; some were equipped with backpacks, canteens and blankets. There was also a small group of youths in black who spoke Cantonese among themselves. They looked weary and badly in need of help. I overheard a young man describing a factional war in his hometown involving machine guns and grenades. He was here to file a petition for assistance from the Central Government.

I must have been standing in line for four or five hours when my turn finally came. A woman in army green peered through a small window from behind her counter. I was tired, but glad I had made it.

The woman listened attentively to my story and took notes. "I am afraid I can't accept this envelope," she said, examining the package and handing it back to me. "We don't deal with unemployment issues here. We're here only to help victims of factional struggles."

I was at a loss for words. There was a sympathetic look on her face. She asked for my father's Revolutionary Worker Death Certificate and reread it carefully.

"Please wait," she said. She left her counter for a minute and came back with a man immaculately dressed in a dark gray civilian suit. The man peered through the tiny window and addressed me slowly and clearly. "Comrade Tsung. I am afraid we cannot help you at this reception post. But in your circumstances, I suggest you mail your letter directly to Premier Zhou's Office." He pulled out a pen and scribbled something on a piece of paper. "Here is the correct address," he said with a smile.

"What happened?" exclaimed my mother when I got home. "What took you so long?"

"Long line," I said. "I'm perfectly all right."

"Let's talk in the safe room," she whispered, pointing to our inner room.

When I finished my story, she shook her head and said, "Why on earth did you go to the State Council? You could've gotten yourself shot or arrested."

"Yeah, it was kind of stupid now that you mention it," I admitted. "But I thought the reception post was inside."

"Well, what are you going to do now?"

"Mail it to this address." I showed her the slip of paper from the man in the gray suit.

"Office of the Premier," my mother read. "They must receive hundreds or even thousands of letters every day. How do you know if anyone will notice yours?"

I thought about it. She was right. I had to grab the attention of whoever opened my envelope.

"You were really lucky the soldier was friendly," my mother remarked. She was still thinking about my close encounter.

"You should've seen the surprise on his face when I told him I was from the U.S.A." We both chuckled.

"And the man in the gray suit was helpful too," she added.

"Wait, I've got an idea!" I said, and got out my father's old Remington typewriter.

"Don't tell me you're going to write your letter in English!"

"Not quite," I replied. "I have something better."

I went through my drawers and pulled out an article I had translated into English. It was one of the last exercises my father had corrected before the Red Guards took him away.

"Why are you sending your translation?" my mother asked.

"Like you said, there are tons of incoming letters at the Premier's Office. But I doubt if his staff often comes across something in English." It was just a small tactical detail. I was certain my father would have liked it.

That night, I typed a clean copy of the translation, and revised my letter for the fifth and last time. My mother stayed up late and asked me to read the final draft to her.

```
Office of the Premier
State Council of the People's Republic
of China

Dear Premier Zhou:

    I am from the United States. I was born in New
York City and came to China with my parents in
1953. My father Tsung Wei-hsien had served in the
Nationalist Foreign Service for more than twenty
years as vice consul, consul, and consul general
in the United States, Cuba, Mexico, Canada and
the Philippines. In August 1953, in response to
the call of the Foreign Ministry of the People's
Republic of China, my father resolutely and
firmly broke away from the reactionary Nationalist
```

regime, and returned to our beloved Motherland. My father died in January 1969; in recognition of his patriotic action, the Beijing Institute of Foreign Trade awarded me a Revolutionary Worker Death Certificate which recognized my father's patriotic repatriation.

Dear Premier Zhou: It is without choice that I write to you in the hope that the Government of New China can help me out of my present predicament. In August 1966, I was dismissed by my school where I had taught college students and foreign trade cadres. The Personnel Department claimed that I was a "contract worker," and that my so-called "contract" had "expired." The truth is I had been transferred to this school to teach English. I will not bore you with the details; the long and short of it is that I have approached several organizations for help, including the Commission for Returned Overseas Chinese Affairs, and they all referred me back to my school. And so I have been essentially without work for almost five years.

My father brought me to China in the hope that I would someday serve the country he loved so dearly. I know that many young people have been mobilized to work in the countryside. It is all part of building New China. My difficulty is that I can not leave my mother who is old and very ill. I myself am not in good health either. But I am well versed in both Chinese and English languages, and I am a qualified language instructor. Moreover, as you can see from the enclosed paper, I am an excellent translator as well. I would like very much to offer my knowledge and skills to the great cause of building our beloved Motherland into a great socialist country and a strong world power which my father had hoped to see so much when he answered your call to return to China.

Respectfully yours,

Tsung Cheng

I mailed it the next morning. It was a long shot. But I had made my move.

Roughly two weeks after my letter went out in the mail, I got a call on a public telephone downstairs. "Comrade Tsung Cheng?" asked a stranger's voice on the other end of the line.

I answered in the affirmative.

"This is the Office of the Foreign Trade Minister Bai Xiangguo. Can you come to our office tomorrow morning at ten o'clock?"

My heart started to pound. "Yes," I replied. "Will the sentry guard let me in?"

"There is a reception booth next to the guard. Just tell the receptionist that Comrade Hua of the Minister's Office is waiting for you."

When I walked into his spacious office the next morning, an officer in a neatly pressed navy uniform rose from behind a huge desk. He had the bearing of a high-ranking officer. "Please be seated," said my host, who introduced himself as Comrade Hua, special assistant to Foreign Trade Minister Bai Xiangguo. The man went straight to the point. "You wrote to Premier Zhou Enlai two weeks ago."

I nodded.

"We have received instructions from the Premier's Office to resolve your problem. Comrade Ye of our Personnel Department is expecting you."

I could hardly believe my ears. I was about to rise from my seat when he inquired about my mother's health.

"I understand that your father passed away in January," he continued. "We have also been instructed by the Premier's Office to provide your mother with a modest *fuxujin*, a pension. This is to take effect immediately."

Comrade Ye turned out to be a young woman cadre. "Welcome to the Ministry of Foreign Trade," she began. "You are now one of our employees."

I was speechless.

"You've probably heard about our farm in Little Hot Spring Mountain," she said. "We've transferred a group of foreign language cadres to this farm. They do part-time language study and part-time farm work. Your assignment is to participate in the labor and help them with their language studies." I had indeed heard about the Ministry-owned farm in the remote suburbs of Beijing and the small group of elite cadres hand-picked by the Ministry.

"A truck comes to the city twice a month," explained Comrade Ye. "It drops you off at the Ministry on Saturday afternoon and you can hitch a ride back to the farm on Monday morning." So there would be no need for my mother to move. I could visit her every other weekend.

It was unbelievable. Against all odds, I had overcome the impossible. Most of the staff and faculty members in my school had been temporarily relocated to a distant village in Henan Province along with their families. If I had not lost my job, my mother and I would have followed them there. But as providence had it, we were spared.

When I returned home to tell my mother, I was reminded of one of my father's favorite Chinese sayings. "When the old man on the frontier lost his horse, who could have guessed it was a blessing in disguise."

"How true indeed," my mother said.

Chapter 19

Breezes from the West

"It's too good to be true," Old Professor Ren sighed as he lay down on his bunk with his arms comfortably outstretched behind his head. We were on the farm in Little Hot Spring Mountain. He was an affable gentleman, a gourmet and extremely fastidious.

"Too good to be true," he repeated in English.

"What do you mean?" I asked.

It was nighttime. The room was quiet. All the foreign language cadres had gone to the Guangzhou Trade Fair to interpret for Chinese foreign trade corporations and foreign businessmen, and there was only a skeleton crew left on the farm with hardly any chores to do.

"Look around you," he continued. "So tranquil. I would not trade anything for this."

"But why 'too good?'" I asked. Actually, I knew what he meant. The old professor did not have to elaborate.

He only laughed and said, "Shall I turn off the light?"

As I lay on my upper bunk staring at the ceiling, I thought about the old professor's words. Little Hot Spring Mountain seemed remote from it all. It was so tranquil, as he had said. And yet, what was really going on out there? I recalled the front page of the *People's Daily* showing American journalist Edgar Snow and his wife standing beside Chairman Mao on the Tiananmen podium on the National Day of 1970. It was an extraordinary event, a signal of some kind, I thought as I drifted into sleep, unaware that more events soon to follow would change the course of my future.

In spring the following year, the whole world was transfixed by an event that became known as Ping-Pong Diplomacy. The American team at the World Table Tennis Championship in Japan, was invited to China. I read about it again and again in the *People's Daily*. It was all over the news and everyone at the farm was talking about it.

It had all started in Nagoya, Japan with a ping-pong player from Santa Monica hitching a ride with the Chinese team. An exchange of souvenirs took place. Almost like the wave of a wand, nine U.S. table tennis players, along with their wives, four officials and three journalists, found themselves in Beijing's Great Hall of the People as honored guests of Premier Zhou Enlai, who declared that the U.S. team had "opened a new page in the relationships between the Chinese and American people." I thought the whole thing was rather incredible. As it turned out, the occasion was much more than a symbol.

Barely three months later, in July 1971, Dr. Henry Kissinger secretly flew to Beijing via Pakistan. A week later, President Nixon announced that he would soon visit China. All work on our farm stopped. We spent hours studying the official documents from the government regarding China's new move toward improved relations with the United States. Even our English study time was spent reading articles by *New York Times* editor James Reston, and Edgar Snow, the first Western reporter to interview Mao Zedong and author of *Red Star Over China.*

For well over a decade, we quoted Mao's famous saying, "The East Wind prevails over the West Wind." He had made this statement in 1957 when the Soviets launched Sputnik I and the Communist camp was one big happy family. But now, for the first time, I felt a gentle breeze from the West. The possibility of returning someday to the United States ran across my mind as I pondered the events.

One late night in September 1971, I was tuning in to the shortwave band with headphones on when a seemingly irrelevant but disturbing story came through. A Trident 1-E aircraft from Communist China had crashed in Outer Mongolia. The Mongolian Government lodged a serious protest over the incident. Nine bodies were found in the wreckage but burned beyond recognition.

I tossed and turned in my bunk, pondering the mysterious air crash. I imagined for a moment that I heard a trijet flying overhead with sonic booms in its trail. Who had been on board? It had to be someone of fairly high rank to be able to fly on a plane, let alone a modern British-made jetliner. The news report was too sketchy, and I could not get it out of my mind.

The October National Day celebrations were canceled, and forty-eight hours later the entire staff of the farm was suddenly transported to the city for an "extremely important" meeting. Everyone kept quiet as our truck rumbled along the road towards the city. When I stopped off at home that afternoon before the meeting, my mother pulled me into our safe room.

"Did you hear about it? Lin Biao is dead!" she exclaimed excitedly. "Killed in a plane crash."

I was startled. "How do you know?"

"Oh, I have my sources," she replied with a mysterious smile.

I told her about the shortwave news. "What was he doing on a plane to Mongolia?" Lin Biao was next in line to Mao's throne. He was cunning. My father once remarked that Lin looked like a vulture waiting for Mao to die.

We exchanged glances and chuckled.

The meeting was held in the old Soviet Exhibition Center outside Xizhi Gate. Workers from the Foreign Trade Ministry and its trade corporations were present to hear the internal announcement from the Party Central Committee. For years, Defense Minister Lin Biao had been Mao's "closest comrade-in-arms" and heir apparent.

But he was pro-Soviet and against U.S.-China rapprochement. It was mind-boggling to hear he had attempted to assassinate Mao and had fled the country after being denounced as a traitor. No mention of pilot error, or whether the plane had been shot down. It was simply suggested that the plane may have run out of fuel. The script read like a thriller. The story was so well concocted that I walked out of the meeting hall with more questions than answers.

"Well? What did you learn about the plane?" my mother asked when I got home that evening.

"Nothing really," I said.

"We will never know the truth, will we?"

I pointed to our walls and whispered into her ear, "The Emperor must have put an end to the Vulture's flight."

On February 17, 1972, the blue and white Spirit of '76 touched down at Beijing Airport. President Richard Nixon extended his hand as he strode eagerly towards Premier Zhou Enlai. It was to be a handshake that would go down in history, and the photograph on the front page of the *People's Daily* was taken at the precise moment when Zhou, standing straight with shoulders back and right hand slightly extended, gave the appearance of reserve, contrasting markedly with Nixon's urgent strides forward and eagerly outstretched hand.

I was mesmerized by this picture. I wished my father had lived long enough to see it. He would have been proud of China. He would have appreciated Premier Zhou's proud stance. He would have told the story once again of how Zhou Enlai's outstretched hand had been spurned by John Foster Dulles at the Geneva Conference in 1954. Today's handshake marked the beginning of rapprochement. I felt good. There was hope after all.

Soon after Nixon's visit, training on our farm ended and all language instructors were transferred back to the foreign trade college. It was good to be back in the city again, and I directed my energy to teaching foreign trade cadres and translating commercial papers from English into Chinese.

Then, an incredible opportunity came knocking on my door.

Part 3

1972-1974

Chapter 20
The Big Door

y jaw must have dropped when I opened our door and saw Hua and his wife, two old school buddies that I'd lost touch with during the Cultural Revolution. There was a broad grin on Hua's face and his wife giggled.

The door across from us squeaked. A pair of glaring eyes peered through a tiny opening. "Just our neighborhood informant," I whispered. "There are four of them in this building, two on each floor."

Hua chuckled. "So that's how the local police are so well informed."

I invited them into our safe room. As soon as we were inside, Hua announced, "We're going to Hong Kong."

"Are you serious?" I said.

Hua's wife nodded and whispered, "We applied for a family visit, but we're not coming back."

Hua was from England and his wife from Indonesia. I was happy for them, although saddened by the prospect of not seeing my good friends again.

"The Big Door's open," Hua declared. "You and your mother must get out of this country while you can."

"How?" I shuddered at the thought of Public Security men banging on our door. I knew that China had begun to permit repatriated Chinese individuals to freely leave the country. But letters were still censored, foreign shortwave broadcasts continued to be jammed, and the terrain was dangerous.

"Don't you have a maternal aunt in Hong Kong?" asked Hua. "If she invites you for a family visit, you can apply for exit permits."

"Letters are censored," I replied. "Too risky."

"That's why we're here," Hua smiled. "We want to help you. We'll contact her when we get there."

I was not expecting such an incredible opportunity. The prospect of crossing Lowu Bridge suddenly became so real that I could not help hesitating. Hua was one of the few friends whom I could confide in and I knew that I could trust him. But one false step could be my undoing.

"I have to think it over," I said.

Hua nodded his head. "There is a new document from the Party Central Committee stipulating that repatriated Overseas Chinese are allowed to leave the country if they choose to," he said quietly. "That's why we dared to apply in the first place."

"How did you find out about this document?"

"At first, through the grapevine. Then my stepfather confirmed it from a reliable source."

"When we first heard about it we were skeptical," said Hua's wife. "But nearly all of our friends have taken advantage of this directive."

"Apply for a family visit!" urged Hua. "That's what we did. We will persuade your aunt to help."

I was still hesitant. Yet I also realized that this might be our only chance.

"Where do we begin?" I finally said.

"Your employer," replied Hua. "And your mother will need to go to the local police station."

"Police!" I blurted with a feeling of dread. "Why the Public Security?"

"I have a good idea," said his wife. "Write to the Returned Overseas Chinese Affairs Office of the Ministry of Foreign Affairs."

"Or better yet, ask your mother to write the letter," Hua added. "Be sure to mention that you're from the United States."

"I need to talk it over with her," I said. "I'll get back to you tomorrow."

After dinner, my mother and I had a good discussion. I added coal to our stove and served Jasmine tea. The building was quiet. We spoke in undertones.

"Hua's father-in-law owns a business in Indonesia," my mother pointed out, "and he probably has a lot of influence in Fujian Province."

"True," I agreed. "But what about it?"

"That's why his family can travel in and out of China freely. Besides, I am pretty certain that your school authorities will stop us."

Everything my mother said was true and made sense. Employers had control over the personal lives of staff members. I winced at the thought of having to deal with the school authorities.

I paced up and down the room. I stoked the coal and sat down again as my mother poured herself some more tea.

It was a tough decision. My mother wanted to leave mainland China just as much as I did. But the stakes were high; we knew that there was no turning back once we started.

And yet I felt something tugging me. It was an unstoppable urge.

"Times have changed," I said. "The Big Door's open."

"Is it wide open?"

"Frankly, I don't know. But China is now at odds with the Soviet Union. The Russians are a superpower with nuclear teeth. China needs an ally, and that's why Mao shook hands with Nixon. Premier Zhou's order to open the door is merely part of the overall strategy to build a global alliance with the West against the Russians."

"You're beginning to sound like your dad." My mother laughed. "He loved to talk about global alliances and balances."

Poor Mom, I thought to myself. First, her husband insisted on returning to mainland China. And now, twenty years later, her son wants to leave China. She was caught between her late husband's wishes for his son to serve China, and her grown-up son's desire for intellectual freedom and human dignity in the West.

"The point I am trying to make is that all of this would not have happened if China did not feel so threatened by the Soviets," I said.

Thoughtfully, my mother lifted her teacup and took another sip.

"The weather is good, but it may change again," I continued. "We've got to take advantage of this window of opportunity. What will happen to the country when Premier Zhou's generation retires? Although Red Guard groups were disbanded not long ago, they are still among us, and their hands are stained with blood. What will happen when their generation takes over the country?"

My mother thought about it for a moment.

"Yes, you're right, my son. There is no future for you here. You have a whole life ahead of you."

She pulled an antiquated suitcase from under her bed, and took out an old envelope.

"Copy this down for Hua," she said. It was the address of Aunt Grace, my mother's younger sister, who was residing in Hong Kong with her husband, Uncle Paul.

My mother came from a tight-knit family, and we were fairly certain that Aunt Grace would not hesitate to help us. But a lot hinged on the willingness of Uncle Paul to go along with the plan, and, even more importantly, there had to be some way for me to find a means of livelihood in Hong Kong. We decided to proceed only if all of our concerns were met. With that, a secret plan was finally hatched.

Hua crossed the border in mid-April 1973. A month later, Aunt Grace's letter arrived. She wrote:

I heard that family members are free to visit each other across the border. In fact, we recently met a young couple from mainland China who are visiting relatives here. Since I am

*ill and cannot travel long distance, Paul and I are inviting
you and Nephew Cheng to visit us in Hong Kong. In fact, all
of our relatives here are also eager to see you both. We have
an extra room in our home, and you are most welcome to stay
with us during your visit.*

When we finished reading the letter, my mother and I looked
at each other. The show was on.

Uncle Wei took off his glasses and laid Aunt Grace's letter on
the table.

"I've been expecting this for some time," he began. "Are you
having second thoughts?"

I shrugged. "Not sure."

"I know that you want to do something useful for China," he
went on, choosing his words carefully. "But let me ask you this: Do
you really think you can unconditionally follow the instructions
of Chairman Mao? Would you obey him even if it meant being
assigned to a work post somewhere in the countryside or some
obscure spot in inland China?"

I thought of my father's wish for me to grow up in his homeland
and contribute to China's rebirth and I wanted to say yes. But, in
the end, I had to shake my head. I honestly could not see myself
blindly obeying the orders of a dictator. I yearned for freedom
and dignity.

Uncle nodded his head sympathetically. "I understand," he said gently. "It is a difficult question. If you can honestly say 'yes,' then you should stay here. If you can't, then you're better off leaving."

Uncle Wei put on his glasses and reread the cursive writing.

"Who's Paul?" he asked.

"My aunt's husband. We couldn't move forward without his support."

"And I guess the young couple must be your friend Hua and his wife."

I nodded.

Uncle Wei smiled. "Your Aunt Grace is even offering a room. A small but good place to start from. How magically wonderful!" He returned the letter to me. "What's your opening move?"

I pulled another letter from my shirt pocket. "Mom wrote this to the Overseas Chinese Affairs Office of the Foreign Relations Ministry. It's still a draft. Can you please take a look at it?"

My mother's handwriting was studiously neat and reserved, almost like a page out of a penmanship book.

Uncle Wei added a few words here and there. He reminded me of my father.

"There. This should do it," he said. "But remember now, her letter will eventually end up in the hands of your school authorities."

"I know," I said. "And that's when the fight begins."

"Whatever happens," he cautioned, "you must not antagonize your school authorities. Stay level-headed and keep on an even keel; try to end on a good note even though you are determined to leave at all costs. Don't burn the bridges behind you."

We continued our conversation for another hour. I went into details of our plans, and how I intended to approach the American

Consulate General in Hong Kong regarding my U.S. citizenship.

Uncle Wei thought for a moment and said, "Hong Kong may be a 'sensual world of flowery temptations.' But material wealth is not everything. You must try to return to the United States at the very first opportunity. Remember: Hong Kong is not your permanent destination."

Chapter 21
Enemies Without Guns

"So you want to go to Hong Kong," my director said with a forced smile, revealing a slightly protruding canine tooth. He put on a genial appearance, but his eyes were hard, cold and wary.

"Comrade Tsung," he continued, "we have invested a great deal in your education and training. You have an important role in our department. I'm afraid I don't see how we can possibly let you go."

I was prepared for this. "It's just a short family visit."

"Hong Kong is on the other side of the border," he said. The gentle accent was now replaced by a slightly harder intonation. "To visit your relatives in the country is one thing, but going to Hong

Kong is quite another."

"I'm sure the school leadership is aware of the Government's open door policy," I replied.

I shifted in my seat uncomfortably as the director stared at me, trying to gauge how determined I was. "I am aware of it," he said evenly. "But besides teaching, you are also doing important translation work for our foreign trade corporation."

I was thrown off guard. Was there something behind his words? When I was first assigned to the corporation, I already had secret intentions of leaving the country. Well aware of the sensitive environment, I was careful to avoid classified papers marked "internal." If I had been reading or translating sensitive materials, the director might use this as an excuse for denying my application to visit Hong Kong. Fortunately, my assignments were commercial letters and papers. The only non-classified translation that came close to technical was an Australian document on food processing and packaging.

"I've completed all my assignments, and they were all commercial," I answered tactfully.

He blinked, but said nothing.

"I only want to visit our relatives in Hong Kong with my mother. She has a heart problem; I must accompany her there."

"Yes, we know about your mother. Perhaps we can arrange for you to accompany your mother to the border town Shenzhen." He smiled and added, "Lowu Bridge is only a few feet long; she'll have no trouble crossing it."

It was so ludicrous.

"You're a veteran foreign trade cadre," I responded carefully.

"You know about the Government's open door policy. What kind of impression would our relatives get if my elderly mother crossed the bridge all by herself while her son was kept behind only a few feet away?"

His face turned slightly red. "No problem. You can tell them that you cannot go to Hong Kong due to work reasons. It is quite common in the West for businessmen to put off their vacations due to company work."

"True. But if I can accompany my mother all the way from Beijing to the border, then why not a few feet across the bridge?"

The director frowned. The conversation was not going anywhere.

"Comrade Director," I said. "I am sure the school leadership will carry out the Party and Government's policy. Can you ask them to carefully reconsider my application?"

He got up and said, "As you wish."

Days went by, and days mounted into weeks. Meanwhile, my aunt had written to my school president. But every time I approached the director, I got the same answer: "No word."

Meanwhile, a new political storm had erupted. The Gang of Four led by Madame Mao launched an anti-Confucius campaign that was really aimed at Premier Zhou Enlai. Big character posters appeared everywhere, and rallies were organized across the country. The tide of fear had set in again. Was the open-door policy in jeopardy? The path my mother and I had started off on had now become even more narrow and dangerous, and the terrain was covered by shifting sands of political strife.

One morning, the director stared at me and announced, "We have an extremely important meeting at one sharp." I had a strange premonition. Five minutes later, two colleagues reminded me to be punctual.

One o'clock. The moment had come. I opened the door to our main office. The room was packed full of faculty members and school officials, the atmosphere tense with anticipation. My mouth felt suddenly dry. I hesitated momentarily in the entrance. A sudden hush gripped the room as I walked in.

The director looked up from behind his desk and stared at me for a second.

"Ahh, here is Mister Tsung at last!" he announced loudly in Chinese, even though I arrived precisely at the time I was told to be there. He emphasized the word "mister" with a hint of sarcasm in his booming voice. I was no longer Tsung *Tongzhi* (Comrade Tsung), but Tsung *Xiansheng*.

He put on a grin, but the smile did not reach his eyes.

"Have a seat." He pointed to an empty chair.

There was a look of mockery in his eyes. Until now, I had respected my director, who was highly competent, and had always been affable to me. But now, I was facing a different person; he had turned into a predator waiting for his quarry to move into position.

My feet felt like lead as I trudged across the room to the chair. High on the wall, a poster read: "After the enemies with guns have been wiped out, there will be enemies without guns."

"Comrades," the director announced, "there is someone

among us who wants to go to Hong Kong. Evidently this person is dissatisfied with our socialist system."

My eyes were riveted to the director's shiny desk. In that instant, it dawned upon me that I had just been branded as an anti-socialist dissident.

"But," he went on, "we are here to help him recognize his mistakes and, hopefully, to change his mind."

The room froze. No one looked at me. Many had their eyes down. It was a well-orchestrated kangaroo court. Although my name was not mentioned, it was clear whom he meant.

As if by signal, Party members and leading cadres rose from their seats and took turns criticizing me, omitting my name in their carefully prepared speeches. A young faculty member spoke about the evils of capitalism and the danger of becoming unemployed in Hong Kong. Then he warned, "American imperialists and their *Kuomintang* (Chinese Nationalist Party) lackeys use Hong Kong as a springboard for launching anti-China activities."

He opened Mao's *Little Red Book* and cited: "Whoever sides with imperialism, feudalism and bureaucrat-capitalism is a counter revolutionary."

Everyone in the room started to chant in a lifeless, ritualistic rhythm, "Long live Chairman Mao! Down with U.S. Imperialism!" My eyes fell on the "enemies without guns" poster. The walls seemed to sway, and my whole body tensed. For a second, I felt like giving up. But I thought of my late father, who had braved the persecutions in spite of his debilitating heart condition.

When the director finally adjourned the meeting, he asked me to join him and his top lieutenants in an adjacent room.

"Well," he said, "did you hear what the revolutionary masses had to say about you? We are quite unhappy about your behavior."

I felt like a novice flung into a boxing ring to face a relentless heavyweight. I knew I was no match for him. My only fighting chance was to survive the stinging blows and get out of the ring.

My first instinct was to remain silent. But I knew he would not let me off that easily. So I chose to sidestep his question. I gave him the one line I had prepared to use over and over again: "Please carry out the Government's policy."

No one spoke.

"Comrade Director," I continued slowly, "we came here for only one reason: we love China. True, we used to live in a capitalist society; but we came to China of our own free will to help build the country. I am sure you know that the Party's policy has always been to welcome us to the Motherland and also allow us to leave freely."

Silence filled the room. The director nervously licked his lips and took out a pack of cigarettes.

"We are aware of the Government's policy," he finally said. "But you need to seriously consider the opinion of the revolutionary masses. You may leave now."

I staggered out of the office building. The wind struck my face as I tromped along the old dirt road to the bus stop. Luckily, there was an empty seat in the back of the bus, and I sank into it as the vehicle pulled away from the curb.

When I got off the bus at South Peace Lane, it was dark. The wind had stopped and I calmed down. I knew there was no turning back. I became even more determined. But I realized that there was a terrible flaw in my original plan: I had failed to make provisions for help in case something went wrong.

"If only I could get hold of Hua," I thought.

Until that moment, I had never believed in divine intervention. But as I approached our gray brick building, Providence gave me the sudden inspiration to visit Hua's stepfather, Old Mr. Shi.

Chapter 22
Divine Intervention

The old man was startled when I showed up at his doorstep. "Come in," he said in a barely audible voice. Short and chubby, he had a large forehead with bushy eyebrows and a contemplative look on his intelligent face.

Mr. Shi was a scientist. While in London, he had been suspected of passing sensitive information to China. Before the British could arrest him, he fled to Beijing with his family. Ironically, during the Cultural Revolution, he was detained on charges of spying for the British. He suffered the same ordeal as my father and had a close brush with death from heart failure. Thanks to the intervention of Premier Zhou Enlai's office, Mr. Shi was released just in time.

"I thought you and your mother were visiting your aunt," said the old scientist as he closed the door.

"Afraid not," I said.

He studied my face for a moment.

"It's such a lovely day," he said. "Come, let's go out for a walk."

As soon as we left the building, he said, "You're in trouble."

"How did you know?"

"It's written all over your face."

I told him about the meeting.

"How awful!" he said. "But take heart. I don't think you're in any grave danger."

"But the anti-Confucius movement . . ." I started to say.

"Mao's wife is no match for Premier Zhou. Unfortunately, Premier Zhou is gravely ill with cancer. But not to fear. He is a great survivor."

"Cancer?!"

"He's hospitalized. Very little information."

"How about his open door policy?" I asked.

"Don't worry, that won't change. We have to thank our Russian neighbors for this one. If it weren't for their nuclear threat, Mao wouldn't have given his stamp of approval at all."

"Then why is my director giving me such a hard time?"

Old Mr. Shi paused to think. "I don't think your director is the only stumbling block. The people who are responsible for your father's detention are probably your obstacle."

We walked on for a little while before turning back.

"Is there any way I can contact Hua?" I finally asked.

"What for?"

"I need help from my Aunt Grace."

"Letters are censored," he said. "But I may have something better."

I was all ears.

"My son Jin is applying for a visiting permit to Hong Kong. If he succeeds, he can contact your aunt."

I was pleasantly surprised.

"Meanwhile, you must remain calm and patient," the old man counseled. "Continue to report to work every day on time. Your conduct must be impeccable. Do not do anything to antagonize your director, but remain firm on your application."

The following day, I met Jin. He was close to twenty. He had a disarming smile, and his searching eyes showed the intelligence of a youth eager to learn and conquer the world. He was artistically inclined and an avid reader of Chinese literature, especially classical poems.

"The message must be by mouth," I began.

"Understood," whispered the young man, like an agent in a cloak-and-dagger operation, and he was enjoying it.

I had spent a couple of days formulating the message in my mind. It had to be simple, but clear enough for Aunt Grace to follow.

"She needs to write directly to the Minister of Foreign Trade," I said.

"Why not higher up?"

"We're prepared to go all the way to the top. But Foreign Trade Minister Bai Xiangguo is the first stop."

I had a list of names and instructions. We went over it several times until I was satisfied that Jin had committed them to memory.

"What about telegrams?" said Jin.

"What about them?"

"They can help push things along." Jin smiled.

I was not sure about telegrams, but no harm trying. "Okay, let's go for it!" I said and shook my young co-conspirator's hand.

To this day, it saddens me when I think of Mr. Shi, who never got to see his son off. One week later, on the day Jin got his exit permit, the family went out to celebrate. Mr. Shi was so excited that he suffered a heart attack. Jin departed for the border shortly after his father's funeral.

Meanwhile, the anti-Confucius storm continued to grow in intensity. But somehow, Premier Zhou, the great survivor, managed to outmaneuver the Gang of Four.

The wind was behind us again. It was time to signal my aunt.

March 1974. My mother and I waited in Temple of Earth Park (Ditan Gongyuan) for our exit permits that took forever to secure.

Chapter 23
The Green Permits

I was about to leave work late one afternoon when my director beckoned me to his office. "The President of our school wants you to know that the Bureau of Public Security has approved your mother's application," he said with a weak smile. "The school leadership is reviewing yours."

The big stick was gone. Until then, I had not heard anything from across the border. But now I knew that my signal must have gone through.

When I got home that evening, I found a letter on the table. "It's from Aunt Grace," said my mother with a bright smile. Her face shone with hope.

It was a carbon copy of Aunt Grace's letter to Foreign Trade Minister Bai. It was written on business stationery with the letterhead "AWT WORLD TRANSPORT" in large English type, and the words "International Air Freight" in four languages: English, French, German, and Spanish.

"Your Uncle Paul owns an international shipping business in Hong Kong," my mother explained.

Addressing the Minister of Foreign Trade, my aunt began: "I am an Overseas Chinese from the United States." I almost fell off my seat when I read this fictitious line. "Must be Jin's idea," I said to my mother, who nodded in agreement.

The last paragraph caught my attention. "Our relatives and friends in the United States all look forward to seeing my sister and her son. We are planning a grand family reunion."

I stared at this paragraph for a long time. It was brilliant!

"What did they say about your application?" my mother asked.

"Your application has been approved by Public Security," I said. "But the school leadership is reviewing mine."

"In that case, it's time to send out my letter," my mother said. She had drafted a letter to Premier Zhou Enlai in case something like this happened. We grinned like schemers onto a new plot.

Two weeks later, my director called me to his office. "Your application is approved. The Personnel Department will help you."

Looking somewhat embarrassed, he added, "It is really not necessary to bring this matter to the top."

I smiled and left.

The Public Security East District Office was packed when my mother and I arrived. A woman officer called our names and led us into a room where there were file cabinets and an old wooden desk stacked high with folders. After a couple of questions, the officer opened a drawer and pulled out two blue-green documents bearing our passport photos and the words: "PASS FOR TRAVELING TO/FROM HONGKONG-MACAO."

"Your travel permits," she said categorically.

I examined the papers: Destination – Hong Kong. Point of exit/ entrance – Shenzhen. Both papers were stamped with red seals of the Beijing City Public Security Bureau. At the bottom were the effective dates: April 25 through September 30, 1974.

"Don't go to Shenzhen before May 30," advised the woman in uniform. My mother and I exchanged glances.

"Hundreds of people from Fujien, Guangdong and other parts of the country are lining up at the same border point with the same permits as yours," she explained. "No use for you to get there early even though your papers are effective now."

"Seeing is believing," I muttered when we got home.

"For Heaven's sake, lighten up!" my mother laughed and held up her Hong Kong pass. "The border is in sight."

"I won't believe it until we're there." I had heard on the shortwave band that there was an exodus at the border point. It was creating a headache for the Hong Kong authorities, who had started to set limits at their end.

"Regardless, let's plan on leaving on the 25th," I said.

"Better inform your aunt." My mother grinned. "Send her a telegram."

Beijing Telegraph Building was the only place in town where I could cable Hong Kong. It was rumored that a senior high school student had tried to call the British Embassy from one of its phone booths. Heaven knows how he came up with such a harebrained scheme. The young man probably got through for a second or two, and even managed to say "hello" in English before he was whisked away by Public Security agents and sentenced to labor camp. The story was a bit far-fetched but enough to keep locals out of the building.

I presented my newly acquired exit permit. The telegraph clerk handed me a form to fill out. There was a space at the bottom for messages in Chinese. Out of curiosity, I asked how Chinese characters were transmitted.

"Chinese characters are transcribed into four-digit codes," the clerk explained. "On receipt, the Hong Kong Cable and Wireless Company transcribes the numerical codes back into Chinese characters."

"Can I send my message in English instead?" I asked. The notion of relying on someone to transcribe four-digit codes did not appeal to me. I did not want to risk the slightest chance of mistakes.

"No problem," the clerk smiled. He gave me another form and pointed to an old typewriter that stood on a small table at the far end of the room. "It's for foreign guests and journalists, but you can use it."

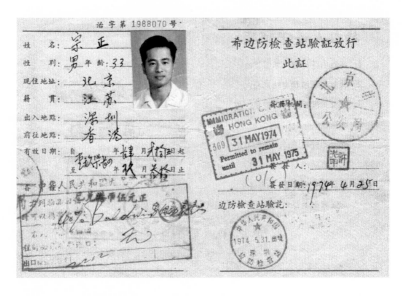

I was probably the only Chinese American to cross Lowu Bridge to British Hong Kong with a Beijing-issued exit permit on May 31, 1974. My name is shown in Chinese characters 宗正 (pronounced *zong zheng*).

The rectangular seal on the lower left shows items of monetary value that I was allowed to bring out of the country: five Hong Kong dollars (after duty) and a battered Swiss Baldwin watch.

持証人遵守事項

1. 此証不得轉借，不得塗改；
2. 持証人須經指定地點出入；
3. 此証只限有效期内使用，逾
   期無效；
4. 此証有效期滿時，須向簽發
   机關繳銷；
5. 此証須妥为保管，如有遺失，
   应立即向簽發机關報告。

往來港澳
通行証

Registered on 10 JUN 1974
for/under H.K. Identity
Card N° 257713
Father
Mother's I.C. No.

for Commissioner of Registration

I drew a lot of attention when the Hong Kong Immigration learned that
I was born in New York City. A British officer interviewed me for half
an hour before the immigration officer affixed the rectangular seal
to my exit permit.

I rolled in the sheet and was just about to type the letter "P" when I felt a vice-like grip on my right shoulder. A man and a woman had come up from behind. It was the man who clamped down on me.

"What are you doing here?" he demanded in a husky voice, flashing his Public Security ID.

I froze. But I managed to pull out my exit permit and replied, "I am an Overseas Chinese going to Hong Kong. The clerk said I could type my telegram in English."

The woman said, "Wait here." She strode over to the clerk. Eventually she waved and said, "Okay, go ahead."

The two Public Security officers withdrew. With a sigh of relief, I typed: "PASSPORTS SECURED ARRIVING EARLY JUNE."

Chapter 24
Farewell

he day of our departure finally arrived. I was filled with excitement; yet, strangely, I also felt a little sad. In spite of all the setbacks and sorrows, Beijing had become my second hometown. I could not bear the thought of leaving my good friends, truly wonderful individuals whom I had learned to trust over the years and would probably never see again. With mixed emotions, I closed our apartment door for the last time, picked up the only suitcase we were taking and set out for the railway station with my mother.

The somber green passenger cars of the International Train number 15 stood at attention like a row of sentries as we padded across the spacious platform of Beijing Railway Station. At the head, a shiny locomotive with eight driving wheels puffed steam and energy, poised for a 7:10 p.m. departure.

Uncle Wei was leaning on a walking stick with his son at his side. Grandma Song and her daughter were also there to see us off. They were among a handful of close friends and relatives who knew that my mother and I were not planning to return. As far as the rest of the world was concerned, we were on a trip south for family visit.

"Remember," whispered Uncle Wei into my ear, "Hong Kong is not your permanent destination. You must try to return to the United States at the first opportunity."

"All aboard," announced the conductor. We boarded the seventh passenger car; the compartment walls were covered with wooden panels and there was ample legroom between the cushioned seats which doubled as beds. Beneath the window was a small fold-in table for tea kettles and cups. An army man and cadre shared the same compartment with us.

I felt a gentle pulling motion. The platform started to slide by our window. Uncle Wei and our friends waved to us for the last time. My mother dabbed her eyes and clasped my arm. "Goodbye my friends," I murmured. "Farewell."

As our train raced along the tracks, my mind was still up north. I missed the winding alleys of Old Beijing. I recalled the sound of peddlers and the rustle of autumn red leaves. I thought of my father and his colorful bedtime stories. I pictured my mentor examining deformed corn stalks on his experimental plot. I smiled at the memory of my first shortwave radio set and the thrill of tuning in to the outside world.

We passed by peasants and water buffalo working in rice fields. A boy and a fisherman drifted by on a small flat boat. The air became increasingly warm and humid as we journeyed southwards. The reality of our departure from Beijing was finally sinking in. Twenty years ago, I was a Chinese-American youngster peering out of a northbound train half curious, half scared. Now, I was a grown man on a southbound train to the border.

I closed my eyes, trying to visualize the Stars-and-Stripes. Would the American Consul believe my story? Or would he suspect that I was a Chinese agent? I could prove my identity, but espionage was quite another matter. After all, I was no longer a twelve-year-old boy but a thirty-three-year-old adult. I could not help noting the irony of it all. In China, my father was suspected of spying for the Americans; and now his son might be suspected of spying for the Chinese. The truth was that neither of us was capable of espionage.

I felt a warm draft on my cheeks when someone opened the compartment window.

"Wake up," said my mother. "We're arriving soon."

I opened my eyes and glanced out the window at the lush growth of subtropical trees and plants. It was hot and muggy. After two days and one night on the rail, we had crossed the Yangtze River, the great water that divides the country into North and South China, and finally arrived in Guangzhou, the capital of Guangdong Province in the deep south.

Chapter 25

Border in Sight

uangzhou's Nanyang Hotel was not exactly first class, but the floors were swept, the sheets smelled fresh, and the beds had spring mattresses. On the ground floor, there was a restaurant packed full of hungry travelers and locals eating, laughing, and chatting in strange nine-tonal syllables. Waitresses pushed little carts loaded with colorful dishes and steaming rice porridge. I felt like a northern barbarian in a well-manicured garden of southern dainties. Instead of water-cooked coarse noodles, we had thin noodles deep fried and toasted. The familiar water dumplings of the North were not on the menu; instead, steamed shrimp dumplings in translucent wrappers served in miniature bamboo steamers were served from carts.

"Cantonese dim sum," my mother exclaimed gleefully. We were in the land of exotic foods. Her eyes lit up. She was back in her element. She even understood the Cantonese waitresses.

While we were in Beijing, we had already learned that no one was allowed to bring Chinese currency out of the country. What surprised us was that the People's Bank only allowed us to exchange Chinese Renminbi for ten Hong Kong dollars, the equivalent of about two U.S. dollars, for buying train tickets from Lowu to Kowloon. But my aunt lived across the harbor from Kowloon, on Hong Kong Island.

"Only ten?" I asked. "Is that all?"

"It'll take you as far as Kowloon station," the clerk replied. "Your relatives can pick you up there."

"My mother has a heart problem," I said. "Can we have a little more for emergencies?"

Smirking, the bank clerk said, "In that case, she shouldn't travel at all."

Train number 93 departed Guangzhou at seven sharp on the morning of May 29 and arrived in Shenzhen in the afternoon. It was a small border town with no hotels except the Overseas Chinese Mansion, which was reserved for travelers with foreign passports.

Since we were traveling as Chinese residents without passports and only had Chinese border passes, our status did not qualify us for the Mansion. We were only allowed to stay at a squalid inn packed with people waiting to cross the border.

There were no cabs or buses. Instead, a pool of suntanned taxi-cyclists lined up in front of the railway station hungry for business. My mother perched on the back of one bicycle, while I sat on the rear of another, clinging to our only suitcase of worldly possessions.

Early the next morning, we went down to the border checkpoint. There was a long queue. We submitted our green passes to the sentry, who gave us tickets with numbers. We reached the gate but missed the quota of the day. We learned that some people had been waiting for days, lining up over and over again; so we prepared ourselves for a much longer ordeal at the inn.

That night, I did not get a bed. Families had to share rooms and there were not enough beds for everyone. The low buzzing of mosquitoes and flies and the horrible stench from the common lavatory kept me awake, sweating on the bamboo mattress on the floor and listening to the distant murmurs of people in the darkness of the night.

"The customs officers are a mean bunch," said a voice.

"So I heard," replied another in some variation of Fukienese language close to my mother's Amoy dialect.

I reached out to touch our small suitcase. It contained nothing of monetary value except for two newly purchased bottles of Maotai liquor. We also had a small silver spoon with a curved handle inside the suitcase. It was my American baby spoon that had somehow eluded the Red Guards during the Cultural Revolution.

I was not worried about the Chinese customs. But I wondered what I would tell the British authorities on the Hong Kong side. Should I reveal my birth certificate? Should I tell them about my plans to return to the States? "If you do," someone had cautioned me, "you will only get a transit visa. Just tell them you were born in China." I gave this a great deal of thought. Since my ultimate goal was to reclaim my U.S. citizenship, I decided to adhere to the truth. Consistency was the surest ground.

It was getting cooler now as a gentle breeze set in. The border was in sight. Tomorrow we would rise with the sun and try again.

Lowu Bridge

Chapter 26
Lowu Crossing

I t was late morning May 31, 1974, when my mother and I finally made it into the Chinese customs house at Lowu border point.

"Line up over there!" growled a border guard who strode into the room and pointed to a long empty bench on our left. He was carrying a stack of exit permits and a box of folders. He called out names one by one, and examined each person's face against the photographs on our exit passes. The room was subdued as the armed officer spent several seconds scrutinizing each individual. My mother was ahead of me. When the officer was satisfied with her identity, he returned her green pass.

Everybody was staring at the floor nervously. The guard stopped in front of me; I looked up at him. With a cold and ugly glare, he asked me in a loud, grating voice: "Name?"

"Tsung Cheng."

"Occupation?"

"English language instructor."

The guard opened a folder and asked, "Why are you going to Hong Kong?"

"Visiting relatives with my mother."

I was the only one in the room questioned by the officer. I glanced at my mother who was waiting apprehensively on the other side of the room. Why was I being singled out for interrogation? I grew suspicious and wondered what was in the folder.

Before I knew it, the guard returned my travel permit. My mother and I proceeded to the customs.

"Are you carrying any Chinese currency?" asked an officer in gray.

We had about fifteen *yuan* left. He pointed to a door and said, "Can't bring the money out of the country. Go through that door."

To my surprise, the room turned out to be a combination of a post office and bank. I emptied my wallet and remitted all we had to my uncle in Amoy, except for three pennies change.

"Can I keep the coins for a souvenir?"

The clerk shook his head. "Against regulations," he said. Pointing to a jar on his counter, he said, "Buy some candy for the road."

The customs officer searched my pockets and scanned my mother with an x-ray machine before we moved on to the baggage inspection area where two more officers were waiting.

"Only one suitcase?"

I answered in the affirmative. Neatly and efficiently, the officer went through the contents of our suitcase, ignoring the two Maotai bottles packed in plain sight. He examined the sterling spoon for a second and put it back in the suitcase.

By now I felt much more relaxed. I knew that we were really on our way out.

"No jewelry?"

I shook my head. "Only a watch," I said. I slipped it off and gave it to him. It was a Baldwin boy's wristwatch my mother had bought for me in New York City two decades ago. He whipped out a magnifying glass but quickly returned it to his pocket. My seventeen-jewel Swiss looked so old and battered that the officer decided that he did not need to magnify it after all. Instead, he wrote on my exit permit: "40% Baldwin *nan zidong biao yi zhi*," which roughly means "one 40% Baldwin male self-winding watch." He estimated that the watch was worth only forty percent of its original value! Actually, it was not even self-winding.

"Are you Overseas Chinese?"

There was a look of disbelief when I told the officers that we were originally from the United States.

"When did you come to China?"

"1953," my mother replied.

"Didn't you have any jewelry or valuables then?"

"I sold all my jewelry and even my wedding ring about twenty years ago."

"What was your husband's occupation in the United States?" asked a senior officer.

When I told him that my father was a Chinese Nationalist

diplomat who had returned to China for patriotic reasons, he shut our suitcase and said, "Okay, they can pass."

"Why did you tell them about Father?" my mother whispered as we walked towards the exit. We had agreed not to tell anyone about him.

"It's okay; we're still on the Chinese side of the border," I whispered.

Two armed Chinese sentries stood at attention outside. No submachine guns. Just rifles. The little wooden bridge that we had crossed twenty years ago was gone. In its place was a small thoroughfare with an arched roof supported by steel-ribbed posts. Two lanes of railway tracks ran from one end to the other. The distance was so short that I could plainly see the faces of the British Hong Kong sentry guards on the other side of the border. A low gray concrete building stood behind the dark blue uniformed sentries, and a large red, blue and white Union Jack fluttered majestically in the breeze.

With ten Hong Kong dollars and a small dilapidated suitcase between us, my mother and I slowly made our way past the Red Flag and green-uniformed guards, and followed the shiny rail tracks toward the Union Jack.

We crossed the boundary point. It was behind us now. Our new journey had begun.

At the entrance to the gray building, I paused for one last glimpse of the other world. In the distance, the Five-Star Red Flag was still fluttering proudly on its tall mast. The two green-uniformed People's Liberation Army sentries were still standing at attention. Lowu Bridge seemed to glitter as my eyes swept the length of the shiny rails. For an instant, I thought I saw my father on the bridge smiling at us. Tears blurred my vision as the tall figure melted into the north.

A gentle westerly breeze brushed my cheeks as if to welcome me. A young Hong Kong Immigration officer in a white shirt and blue necktie stood by the opened door. Suddenly, I felt a surge of exhilaration.

I looked at my mother and she looked at me. Arm in arm, we entered the immigration outpost.

Epilogue

April 1, 1956

Dear aunt Mary:

I am not fooling you. But this looks like my aunts week. I got a letter from aunt Anor from London, a letter from my grand aunt (Lin) from France, a can of Hills Bros. coffee from my aunt in Foochow (in southern China), and lastly a letter from you plus stamps. It's indeed a nice feeling to have aunts, good aunts, aunts who remember their far-away nephew. It is touching to think of and to be thought of by those dear to you. I sound as though I were too sentimental for a boy, but I can't help it.

Now, on this All Fools' Day in China tricks are not being played. Only we are being tricked by Old Man Weather. He doesn't seem to have made up his mind yet whether to give us spring or leave us in winter. It is still cold and damp besides. The Hills Bros. coffee in such a weather, however, comes in handy. But how I wish I could have a couple of hot dogs with it. Somehow or other I have developed an appetite for everything eatable. Father says that "to eat" in my vocabulary should be a regular verb rather than irregular, because every time I come home I just eat, and eat and keep on eating until I leave for school and even then I usually bring along with me a roll of butter, half a dozen hard-boiled eggs and a jar of peanut butter. But then father has to admit that I haven't been eating for nothing, for I've grown quite a bit -- almost as tall as he now.

A letter to Aunt Mary, April 1 1956

School life is getting more and more active. You
always
can∧tell by my shoes -- again father says, because the
heels wear off so fast. Well, you can't blame the old
man for being so observing; after all, it is he who has
to pay for the cobbler's smiles.

Mother, the cook, the maid, the laundress, and the
typist all in one, just works and works. Her only re-
creation is to go with me to father's school mm to see a
picture every week-end -- the show is free.

Father as usual loves to read. He is reading Samuel
Johnson and Shakespeare. Since he came back, he has translated a couple of books, and believe it or not, he is working
on his monkey story. There is a chance that he may get it
published.

Is there anything you can send over to me? Yes, if
you don't mind my being too monotonous. I like to get a
copy of Sears Roebuck or Montgomery catalogues Do you
think you can find me a copy? I want to keep it for reading purposes, because I've forgotten so many little things
about the household life in the U.S. I hope I am not asking too much.

How are your folks? Have you heard from aunt Vi?

Love
Cheng

year after our crossing Lowu Bridge into Hong Kong, I managed to track down Aunt Mary and visit her in Oklahoma City. She was in her eighties, her red hair had turned silver, but I recognized the same wit and humor.

"What happened after you saw us off at Grand Central?" I asked.

"I drove out west as planned. After settling in with my father, I decided to try out your aunt's address. When I got your first letter, I was so delighted. I knew that our letters would be read by someone else, so I visited the local FBI office and told them about my intention to correspond with you."

She poured herself a cup of black coffee and chuckled. "You should have seen the face of the young agent when I said, 'I'm not a Communist and I'm not a sympathizer either. But I intend to correspond with this twelve-year-old Chinese-American youngster.'"

Aunt Mary paused and stood up. "Let me show you something." I followed her into the living room. Next to her armchair, there was an old photograph of eleven-year-old me in my Civil War Union

army hat and I watched as she opened an old leather trunk. I stared in disbelief. All of my letters from Beijing were neatly bundled together. I picked them up and examined the old envelopes and letters, some handwritten in my childish penmanship, and others typed on my father's old portable – a time capsule from a distant past now in my hands.

"Although the letters were yours," she said, "I could always tell which parts were really from your father, and I got a pretty good sense of how things were with you and your parents."

"How?"

Aunt Mary winked. "Reading between his lines." She took a letter out of an envelope and pointed to the postscript. "Here. You'll see what I mean."

I read my father's words. *I don't think there's much to add on my part except perhaps a little apology for this ribbon, which, as you can easily see, is fast "fading away" like its owner.*

"See it now?" she smiled.

Behind my father's joking tone, the words "fading away" were meant to give Aunt Mary a veiled picture of our life in Beijing without sounding dissatisfied with the Chinese government.

"You know what," I said. "I think I ought to write a book."

Aunt Mary got up from her chair and fetched a little paperback book. The cover was battered at the edges; the pages were dog-eared and starting to yellow. It was the third edition of *The Elements of Style* by William Strunk, Jr. and E.B. White.

"Use it well," she said. "And good luck."

The return address on the upper left corner of the envelope is my school, Peking Returned Overseas Chinese Preparatory School. The Chinese characters on the lower left side read: 寄到美国 Mail to U.S.A.

Acknowledgments

I should begin by thanking Celeste and Chok Yu, who persuaded me to pick up my pen and start writing. I was a novice, but Celeste kept pushing me harder.

I am especially grateful to my good friend Genevieve Dean for transcribing my tapes and reading and rereading my initial manuscript and all its iterations, and pressing me with difficult and soul-searching questions.

I am indebted to Carol Ann Bergman who took time to comment on my work.

This book would not have become a reality without Passager Books editors Kendra Kopelke and Mary Azrael. I am grateful for their recognition, and truly honored. It has been a pleasure to work with them, and their very special assistants, Saralyn Lyons and Ashley Phelps.

Special thanks to Pantea Amin Tofanghchi for her artistic work, her enthusiasm and all the thoughtful ideas that went into the elegant book design.

I also want to thank my good friend Charles Ku for the Chinese characters 一线之隔; Ms. Yifei Hu, who created the calligraphy for the chapter numbers; and Mr. Guoqiang Zhang for consulting about the calligraphy.

I treasure the warm support of Jack Swenson, my creative writing instructor at the Fremont Senior Center, and my fellow classmates who listened patiently while I read chapters of my work-in-progress. I am very fortunate to be among writers and poets who write with generosity, creativity and humor.

Sincere thanks to Dr. Douglas Murray, my former director at Stanford University's U.S.-China Relations Program, and Dr. Thomas Fingar, my former colleague in the U.S.-China Relations Program.

Finally, I must express my heartfelt gratitude to my wife Blesila and my daughters Kristine and Lauren for their loving support, and for sharing my dream of finding a wider audience for my story.

Beyond Lowu Bridge was designed and typeset and illustrated by Pantea Amin Tofangchi. The text pages are set in Adobe Garamond Pro and Optima.

The cover art is acrylic on rice paper by Pantea Amin Tofangchi.

The Chinese calligraphy was done by Yifei Hu.

In legends, the crane stands for longevity, peace, harmony, good fortune and fidelity. A high flyer, it is cherished for its ability to see both heaven and earth. These ancient, magnificent birds, so crucial in the wild as an "umbrella species," are now endangered and must be protected.

Passager Books is dedicated to making public the passions of a generation vital to our survival.

Also from Passager Books

A Cartography of Peace
by Jean L. Connor

Improvise in the Amen Corner
by Larnell Custis Butler

A Little Breast Music
by Shirley J. Brewer

A Hinge of Joy
by Jean L. Connor

Everything Is True at Once
by Bart Galle

Perris, California
by Norma Chapman

Nightbook
by Steve Matanle

I Shall Go As I Came
by Ellen Kirvin Dudis

Keeping Time:
150 Years of Journal Writing
edited by Mary Azrael & Kendra Kopelke

Burning Bright:
Passager Celebrates 21 Years
edited by Mary Azrael & Kendra Kopelke

Hot Flash Sonnets
by Moira Egan

gute -